THE Cape

FINDING LITTLE ME

THE

FINDING LITTLE ME

Amy Agnew Irvine

Copyright © 2024 Amy Agnew Irvine. All rights reserved.

Illustrations contributed by Katherine Haff

No part of this publication may be reproduced, stored in a retrieval system or transmitted in any form or by any means, electronic, mechanical, photocopying, recording or otherwise, without prior permission of Halo Publishing International.

The views and opinions expressed in this book are those of the author and do not necessarily reflect the official policy or position of Halo Publishing International. Any content provided by our authors are of their opinion and are not intended to malign any religion, ethnic group, club, organization, company, individual or anyone or anything.

For permission requests, write to the publisher, addressed "Attention: Permissions Coordinator," at the address below.

Halo Publishing International
7550 W IH-10 #800, PMB 2069,
San Antonio, TX 78229

First Edition, October 2024
ISBN: 978-1-63765-678-5
Library of Congress Control Number: 2024919469

The information contained within this book is strictly for informational purposes. Unless otherwise indicated, all the names, characters, businesses, places, events and incidents in this book are either the product of the author's imagination or used in a fictitious manner. Any resemblance to actual persons, living or dead, or actual events is purely coincidental.

Halo Publishing International is a self-publishing company that publishes adult fiction and non-fiction, children's literature, self-help, spiritual, and faith-based books. We continually strive to help authors reach their publishing goals and provide many different services that help them do so. We do not publish books that are deemed to be politically, religiously, or socially disrespectful, or books that are sexually provocative, including erotica. Halo reserves the right to refuse publication of any manuscript if it is deemed not to be in line with our principles. Do you have a book idea you would like us to consider publishing? Please visit www.halopublishing.com for more information.

*For my mom, Susan Agnew,
my biggest cheerleader,
For my children, Emily and Colby Irvine,
my greatest inspirations and magic,
For my younger selves,
we did it!*

*Once you've gotten to know
your younger selves,
it's a lot harder
to let them down...
~Midlife Amy*

Contents

The Prologue		13
Part 1 ~ Little Me		**21**
Chapter 1	Little Amy	23
Chapter 2	The Cape	27
Chapter 3	Choices	33
Chapter 4	The Tomboy	37
Chapter 5	The Little Adult	43
Chapter 6	The Overachiever	51
Part 2 ~ Early Adulting		**61**
Chapter 7	Sorority Aim	63
Chapter 8	London Calling	71
Chapter 9	Twenty-Something	79
Chapter 10	And What Do You Do?	87
Chapter 11	Super Mommy	95
Part 3 ~ Serious Adulting		**109**
Chapter 12	Single Mom	111
Chapter 13	The Cape Turned Pink	123

Chapter 14	The Slow, Quiet Crash	133
Chapter 15	Hugging the Kryptonite	141

Part 4 ~ Midlife Awakening   **151**

Chapter 16	Finding Little Amy	153
Chapter 17	Layers	159
Chapter 18	The Test Flight	171
Chapter 19	The Sabbatical	181
Chapter 20	New Habits	193

Part 5 ~ Future Me   **205**

Chapter 21	The Reentry	207
Chapter 22	One Sunny Day on a Lake	213
Chapter 23	The Big, Audacious Dream	219

The Epilogue	225
Acknowledgments	239
Let's Connect	247

The Prologue

When I was a little girl, I was obsessed with the comic book character Wonder Woman. She represented the first female superhero for my generation of girls and boys. And I wanted to be just like her.

In the 1970s television series, Wonder Woman didn't walk around wearing a cape, her magic powers on display. No, she appeared to be Diana Prince, a typical 1970s nine-to-five working woman. But when someone needed help, Diana removed her glasses and looked for a private location to activate her magic. As she spun around in a circle with her arms out (*Cue music.*), her hair fell out of its bun, and magically, she transformed into my hero.

Along with her supercool red boots and headband, Wonder Woman wore a gold belt and bracelets that deflected bullets. She also carried a magic lasso that she threw to grab the bad guys before they could escape. But, for me, it was Wonder Woman's cape that signified her hero status. And since I wanted to be a hero too, I needed a cape.

Little did I know that, at a rather young age, I would become a real-life hero. During a rather scary event, I reacted bravely and with courage—just like Wonder Woman.

My vivid imagination manifested my superpowers in the form of a shiny blue-satin Cape.

As a child, I used the Cape to fuel my curiosity, challenge my capabilities, and test drive my dreams. My Cape gave me the confidence to try anything that I felt curious about—especially on the rare occasions when I was told no.

My range of magical superpowers expanded as I grew older. The Cape gave me courage in the face of fear. And I grew up to believe in my fearlessness. Of course, I did. I wore a hero's Cape, after all.

Succeeding with magic at a young age was exciting, but it also brought unexpected burdens. Everyone, including me, thought I could do anything, and I was expected to be a superstar at everything I tried. Of course, those expectations only fueled my resolve.

I lived a childhood of daring to try everything—performing, succeeding, and overachieving. My many, many tries resulted in countless trophies and awards, positive feedback from the people around me, and endless future goals. I had tons of confidence in my capabilities.

So why did I have low self-esteem?

Certainly, many social influences impacted my self-worth, including my gender and the social era in which I was raised. The women's liberation movement greatly influenced a society of women wanting to have it all—a family and a career. The female role models of the time reflected a society that was not ready for women to be both smart and pretty, athletic and feminine, powerful and maternal.

On top of those influences, it took years of therapy for me to understand the connection between my low self-worth and my tumultuous, toxic relationship with my father.

I spent my childhood trying so darn hard to be *enough*…at everything. To exceed expectations so that my dad would prioritize me, want to spend time with me, and love me. But he rarely acted like my parent. I never asked him for help; he could not be relied on. I was never enough for him—nor was he for me.

Not having a reliable father or a loving paternal relationship remains one of the saddest deficiencies in my life—even now as an adult. I have spent decades trying to come to terms with and accept this loss, and process and heal from the pain and disappointment it brings. I can't control the sadness, just as I couldn't control my father, the narcissist. I am learning to give myself grace and compassion when the sadness arrives. Acceptance can be hard-won.

In my earlier years, I balanced overachieving with my innate desire to prove my capabilities—and, often, to prove others wrong. My response to an absence of role models was to cultivate a strange confidence in my ability to figure things out. I was the fourth-grade girl who played basketball and football with the boys at recess. I didn't have money for college, so I applied to every scholarship fund I qualified for—and won them all. I didn't have a car in college, so I Rollerbladed to classes. If no one else was doing it, I was even more motivated to try it…and crush it.

But as happens, my attempts became less risky, less self-focused; more calculated, weighed, and considered with age. Rather than live as the hero of my own story, I grew up wearing the Cape to be everyone else's hero. Perfection became my endgame.

Yes, as a young person, I was the Super Achiever hero in the classroom, on the tennis court, on the job, and for my family; the proof was in the accolades and praise. But, decades later, I became a Super Survivor. A hero who endured the plot twists of my life, the impossible superhero persona I created, and the unrealistic magic that my life expected from me.

I suffered as much as I soared while wearing my Cape. And I thought that heroes had to do everything all by themselves. It took many decades for me to realize something very important about superheroes—none of them are invincible; they all have weaknesses.

Whenever Superman encountered the poisonous green kryptonite, he was left powerless, even while wearing his cape. Thankfully, in the DC Comics, Superman had his Super Friends. He was a member of the Justice League—a team of superheroes. And whenever he needed help, other superheroes like Wonder Woman and Batman came to his assistance.

He didn't have to do it all by himself. None of those superheroes did. Such a late-life lesson for me to finally learn. *Wearing a Cape doesn't mean you can't ask for help...*

Of course, my Cape didn't come with an instruction manual. And I didn't find a Cape coach until my early adult years. I spent so much of my early life trying to channel my superpowers, all by myself, with a visceral need to prove that I didn't have to rely on anyone else. My kids even bought me a LEGO

Mother's Day Gift from Amy's children, Davis, California, May 2010.

Wonder Woman key chain for Mother's Day one year. And after twelve years of raising my kids alone, even the LEGO me looks pretty tattered.

For so much of my life, I doubted I was worthy enough to be helped. Everyone knew me as Super Mom. So how could I admit that I wasn't actually Wonder Woman? I tried desperately to maintain my superhero reputation at all costs. Until, that is, no Cape or magical powers could help me save the day.

No matter how well you have tried in life—whether in parenting, working at a job, or loving another person—shit happens. And as a parent, no matter how well you have tried to parent or how well-equipped your children are, the unexpected will happen.

And no one can prepare you for the fact that once your kids start their journey into young adulthood, their story's plot is no longer yours to create or live. Even when you can see that they need a superhero to save them. Sometimes, they just need to save themselves.

During the first week of December 2021, in the midst of a global pandemic, my worst nightmare nearly became a reality. I couldn't take care of my young-adult son's crisis. I couldn't fix it. My body and mind attempted to function while operating at a category-five threat level. Every morning for weeks upon weeks, I woke up weighed down by a heavy fear I'd never allowed myself to imagine, and that fear persisted.

It was a season of no superpowers for this Cape-wearing Wonder Mom. I couldn't figure out how to fix it by myself—nothing I did was working. And so, for the first time, I had to accept the effects of my kryptonite and ask for help. While this slow, quiet crash was probably the scariest thing to happen to me, it led to likely the greatest transformation of my life. The experience has been so life-changing that I wondered if someone else could learn from what I went through. By reading my story, maybe someone else will relate and finally feel seen. And so I began to write.

This is the story of my Cape—the one that I wore for more than four decades of life. The one I thought I could never take off in order to stop being everyone's hero and start being my own. The Cape that allowed me to discover my superpowers and navigate life with sheer determination to thrive through overachievements, successes, failures, and a lifetime of criticism from my very mean inner critic.

Throughout this journey, you will witness the plot twists and pivotal moments that have made up the plot of my life. I'm certain you likely have experienced your own share of plot twists—those radical events that change the direction of a story. And during a plot twist, you are usually left with choices that represent pivotal moments in your life. Those big and little moments of choice, and often clarity, that provide us with new perspectives and opportunities to change our lives. It is within my plot twists and pivotal moments that you will see my Cape grow, both in capabilities and weight.

As you read about my quest to find Little Amy, I hope you'll think about your own little self. *How is your Cape of Capability these days? Is it helping you live your best, most authentic life? Or is it no longer serving the current—or future—you?*

Keep in mind that, in the early chapters, you are reading reflections of a younger person—a child. Memories can be foggy. Imaginations can be grand. The truth may lie somewhere in between.

Now, with the stage set, I hope you enjoy the journey. I'll see you on the other side.

Part 1 ~ Little Me

Part 1 – Little Me

Chapter 1

Little Amy

Once upon a time, there was a little girl named Amy. She loved her family, her friends, the sunshine, and the ocean. Most days, you could find her running, jumping, playing, and dreaming. But, most especially, she loved to read.

From *Goodnight Moon* and *The Giving Tree*, to books by Dr. Seuss and Nancy Drew, she loved stories that ignited her imagination. They transported her to incredible worlds and characters, and filled her mind with wonder, curiosity, and possibilities.

Little Amy especially loved reading stories about great adventures, with hero characters who overcame challenges against the odds. Through these stories, she learned what it meant to act with courage, to persevere, and to do things that people didn't think possible. When her heroes overcame challenges, she believed, *I can do that, too!*

Stories of princesses being saved by princes bored Little Amy. She wanted to be the hero. Her first movie in a theater happened to be *Star Wars* (yes, Little Amy lived in a time long, long ago). She loved the robot R2D2, but she was enamored by Princess Leia. It was the first time that

Little Amy had seen a female hero—a heroine. She wanted to be Princess Leia—courageous, smart, and fearless—and even dressed up as the princess that Halloween.

As she grew older, Little Amy discovered a television (TV) show called *Wonder Woman*. The main character, Diana, was a beautiful, strong woman who was also powerful and fierce. She looked like a regular person until someone needed her help. Wonder Woman then spun around, and suddenly she was a superhero with magical powers that made her helpful to the world (she even helped grown men and police officers). She wore a cape and carried a magical lasso and a shield. Little Amy dreamed of what it would be like to be Wonder Woman.

It will come as no surprise that Little Amy grew up believing that she could be the hero of her own story. When Little Amy wanted to try something new, her mommy almost always said yes. She was lucky to try so many new things and to discover her talents and capabilities at such a young age.

Amy Sue Agnew, Alamo, California, June 1977.

She took dance lessons—and not just one kind. She learned ballet, tap, and jazz. She joined a competitive swim team and won many races. And while watching Tracy Austin and Chris Evert play tennis on television, she begged her parents to let her play. So her dad cut down a tennis racquet to make it small enough so she could take lessons and play, too; they didn't have kid-sized racquets back in those days.

Little Amy felt confident in her abilities. Adults called her capable, and she certainly wasn't afraid to try new things. She didn't yet understand the concept of failure. She just felt excited about life and all the magic she could create in the world around her. She was definitely a fearless little girl. She believed she could try and do anything, and she did.

Until one day, for the first time, she felt very afraid; her mind and body were consumed by fear. And those feelings were certainly justified.

Everyone will feel fear at some point in their lives. Do you remember what you were afraid of when you were your little self? Little Amy's first experience just happened to be on her seventh birthday.

Chapter 2

The Cape

June 1978, an affluent country club in Northern California

Now, this part of the story might feel a little scary. But I want you to remember that Little Amy is okay. It's important to understand Amy's first experience with acting fearlessly and reacting courageously in the face of fear. This was the first time she felt like a real hero. So let's be brave as we walk through this part of the story together.

Little Amy's seventh birthday began like any other summer day in the Agnew household. After breakfast, Amy and her mommy drove her little brother, Randy, to summer camp. When they returned home, Amy played in the family room while her mommy spoke to a friend on the phone. Suddenly the doorbell rang. Little Amy's mommy asked her to go see who was at the front door.

When she got to the door, Little Amy peeked through the window on the right side of the front door. She recognized Ricky, the teenage boy who lived next door. She ran back to tell her mommy who it was. Her mommy ended the phone call and walked with Little Amy to open the front door.

Between the time that Little Amy looked out the window and then returned with her mommy, the young man had pulled a mask over his face. When they opened the door, they saw he was carrying garden shears in his hand. He demanded that Little Amy and her mommy move back, and then he pushed his way into the house.

Little Amy found herself leaning against the living room sofa, in shock, while her mommy screamed, "Ricky, what are you doing?"

Little Amy stood in a state of disbelief. *Is this a television show? This can't be really happening.* She couldn't process what was happening or why the young man was in her home.

The man shouted at her mommy, directing them to move towards the back of the house.

And at that moment, Little Amy felt very, very afraid.

Why did our neighbor put on the mask? What does he want? Is he going to hurt me or my mommy?

Little Amy's mommy smartly chose to back up towards the living room, leading Ricky into the family room near the backyard, rather than to the bedrooms. Suddenly, he pushed her mommy over an ottoman in front of the sofa.

Mommy screamed, "Amy, RUN! RUN!"

Hearing her mother's terrified voice, Little Amy froze, in shock, realizing that she and her mommy must be really in danger. Over the sound of her racing heart, Little Amy realized she could hear the leaf blower in the backyard. Their landscaper, Charles, was just outside!

Amy looked back at her mommy, who was pleading for her to get out of the house. So she ran as fast as her little seven-year-old legs could carry her...straight to the back door and out through the garage to get Charles's help.

The masked man, Ricky, apparently heard the leaf blower, too. He saw Little Amy make it to the garage door, got scared, and ran out the front door.

Little Amy's mommy was very, very brave. She ran after the man, locked the front door, and called the police.

As on the TV shows that she watched, in the end, everyone was okay, safe, and sound. Police officers, neighbors, and family arrived. They told Little Amy that she had been incredibly brave. Her grandparents showered her with lots of love and attention and called her a little hero. Later, she wondered if it all really happened, or was it just a dream? Or maybe it was just an episode of the show *Wonder Woman*?

That afternoon, Little Amy's family headed to their country-club pool to take swim-team photos. Before they left the house, Amy went into her bedroom to put on her racing swimsuit, and she discovered something so amazing that it would change her life forever.

Standing in front of the mirror, her jaw dropped when she saw her reflection. Tied around her neck hung a little, shiny blue Cape. Staring in awe, she cried, "Where did this come from?"

Unable to contain her excitement, Little Amy ran into her brother's room to show him the Cape. "Look, Randy! I have a Cape...just like Wonder Woman!"

Her brother, who was only four years old, really wanted to believe his sister. But, sadly, he couldn't see it.

Baffled, she ran into the bathroom to look in a different mirror. And there it was! The Cape was really there and still draped around her shoulders. But why couldn't Randy see it, too?

Next, she ran to the kitchen to show her mommy—surely, she'd see it!

But her mommy gave her a hug and said, "Amy, you are very brave, and you have a wonderful imagination."

Little Amy felt confused and excited, all at the same time. SHE could see it. Everyone had told her that she had acted with great courage. Is this a Cape of Courage? Staring at the Cape, she thought, *I have a Cape…and it must be magical. So I must be a superhero!*

When she arrived at the swimming pool that afternoon, everyone on her swim team wanted to talk to Little Amy. They told her how courageous she was, and they wanted to hear the story of her bravery. She very much wanted to tell people that it was really the power of her Cape, but she thought they'd think she was crazy. No one could see it.

After the team photos were taken, it was her turn to take individual swim photos. The photographer guided her onto the swim block and told her to imagine she was about to dive into the pool for a race.

Without a swim cap or goggles, she smiled her biggest smile, relishing the attention she was receiving. People were calling her a hero, just like the characters in her favorite stories.

Back in those days, no one really talked about traumatic events, such as the home invasion that Little Amy experienced. The adults assumed that, since

Amy Sue Agnew, Round Hill Country Club, Alamo, California, June 1978.

she was not crying, Little Amy was fine and would soon forget about it, like a television episode; she would only remember it as the time she was very brave.

But the trauma and burden of that experience on the morning of her seventh birthday would impact the rest of Little Amy's life...and every birthday thereafter. It was on that day, when she turned seven years old, that she was certain she discovered her Cape of Courage and knew—in her heart and mind—that she could never take it off. She felt she would always need it to protect herself and the people she loved.

With the burden of the Cape in her mind, Little Amy unwittingly turned into what is called a people pleaser. And not just any people pleaser—she was determined to be the best people pleaser ever. She had a Cape, and she was going to be everyone's hero. Even when that meant taking on the weight of her parents' very adult problems at a very young age.

The home invasion was the first plot twist in Little Amy's life. At the time, she didn't realize how it would send her life on a totally different trajectory than the one of the safe, easy life of privilege that she was living the day before her seventh birthday.

Plot Twist

And in the year that followed, Little Amy and the Cape soared far and high together. To her family, she was still the same positive, driven, and happy child. She performed fearlessly on stage in dance recitals, competed in spelling bees, won tennis matches, and competed in Easter-egg hunt foot races. Little Amy even had her poems published in a school-district book of top writers from kindergarten through sixth grade. She showed no signs of a child recovering from trauma.

Chapter 3

Choices

Two months before her eighth birthday, Little Amy's world rattled yet again. But, this time, it wasn't just an earthquake… It felt like a full-blown plot "twister."

The moving van arrived on Easter Sunday. There would be no egg-hunt race at the country club this year. Her family was moving to a new house, in a new town, away from everything that resembled Little Amy's life.

While her mommy made it sound like an exciting new adventure, Amy couldn't imagine a life that was better than hers. She loved her life, her school, her friends, her dance studio, and her fun sports at their country club. Yet she promised her mommy that she would be her optimistic and fearless self, and embrace the changes with a smile (and her Cape, of course).

As her family drove away from their sprawling ranch house that backed up to the seventeenth hole at their private golf club, her life of privilege quickly disappeared in the rearview mirror. This plot twist would upend her life even more than the unexpected visitor on her seventh birthday. Surely, her life would've been completely different had the country-club house remained her home.

When her family arrived at the new townhouse, the moving van had already arrived. Excited about having a two-story house for the first time, she ran up the stairs to see her bedroom. Her furniture was already in place—the bed just needed sheets and her favorite blanket, pillow, and stuffed animals.

She glanced out her new bedroom window to see two men closing the big moving van's door. *Wow, that was fast!* She spun around and headed out of her room to check out their gigantic new playroom. She smiled when she saw it, imagining all the fun that she and her brother could have playing games and watching TV in this new house.

But by the time Little Amy found and began to explore her parents' new bedroom, a stab of worry filled her stomach. As she looked around, something just didn't quite feel right. Their big king-sized bed was there, so were the nightstands and her mommy's big, long dresser. It was then that she realized her daddy's dresser was missing. And the moving van was empty. Her intuition told her that more was changing besides the new house. Her gut was sadly correct.

She found her mommy in her brother's new room, putting sheets on his bed. "Mommy, where is Daddy's dresser? It's not in your bedroom."

Her mommy sighed and called for her daddy, who was downstairs, talking with her grandparents. Daddy walked upstairs and met Amy, her brother, and their mommy on what would become her mommy's bed.

Plot Twist

Little Amy's parents were getting a divorce. Her daddy would be living in an apartment near her new townhouse. Once more, in the same calendar year, Little Amy was shocked and confused. As understanding began to slowly dawn in her mind, she suddenly felt very, very sad.

And for the first time since her seventh birthday, she felt very afraid. Her head started to hurt so much that she wanted to cry, and her stomach felt as if she might throw up. She felt awful. Little Amy didn't understand why her daddy would want to live somewhere without the rest of the family. She wondered, naturally, *What did I do wrong?*

Her parents did their best to have one of the hardest conversations parents can have with their children. But with reality setting in, Little Amy began to cry. Then her brother cried because Little Amy was crying. Her world felt as if it were crumbling apart. It would certainly never be the same.

Overwhelmed with worry, Little Amy felt as if she needed to be alone. She got up off the bed and went looking for her new bathroom—the one she would share with Randy for the next decade of their lives. While looking for a box of tissues to wipe her tears away, she glanced in the mirror and paused. Beyond her sadness and tears, she was shocked to realize that her Cape was still miraculously on her back. While she felt relieved to see it, she wondered why she still felt so sad, afraid, and overwhelmed.

These scary feelings were very unfamiliar to Little Amy. She was used to being her happy, smiling, optimistic little self. And as she reached back to grab the Cape's edges, she realized that it felt heavier. Could it be that fear, rejection, and doubt had attached themselves to the fabric? She glared at these new additions. And as hard as she tried, she couldn't shake them off.

Holding the Cape, she remembered that it had once helped her feel courageous during a very scary situation. It also gave her a belief in herself when she was unsure about trying something new. Then she did feel the strength of the Cape as a look of determination came into her eyes. She didn't know what was going to happen next, but she wanted to make the sad go away so she could feel like her happy and adventurous little self.

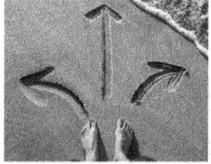

Pivotal moment

At almost eight-years-old, Little Amy made a very important decision: she chose to believe in her strength and the happy life she wanted to live. In that moment, while facing a very big turning point in her life, she demonstrated her authentic resilience.

She chose to be optimistic and focus her mind on all of the excitement that her family's changes brought to her life: a new bedroom to decorate; new neighborhood, school, and friends; and lots of new things to try. She was determined to fly, even with the strange new weight on her Cape.

And it didn't take long before she discovered that in her new town, people still thought she was a fast runner, a smart student, and a kind friend. Her mommy continued to support Amy's eager curiosity and fearlessness, letting her try out for a school musical and even roller-skate in a town parade! It was a yes for countless things to try. Her mother was happy to let her spread her wings and feel like the fearless girl that was her daughter. That is, until one sad day when she actually told her, "No, Amy, you cannot."

Amy Sue Agnew, Walnut Creek, California, June 1979.

Chapter 4

The Tomboy

Little Amy wanted to play soccer, just like her brother and all of the neighborhood kids. Her. mommy never said she couldn't try something. So it's no surprise that Little Amy was surprised by the no.

"But why not?" Little Amy asked in shock.

Mommy explained that soccer was a contact sport. Unlike tennis, swimming, dance, and golf, she could get hurt from running into one of the other soccer players. And if we're going to be real about her mother's reasoning, it wasn't something sweet, feminine little girls did back in those days. This was the late 1970s and early 1980s—girls participating in organized sports was still a new thing and being met with much social resistance.

Frustrated by the no, Little Amy's mindset quickly turned into determination. And after watching one of her brother's soccer practices, Little Amy thought, *Oh, I know I can do that!* She just needed to find a way to change her mommy's mind.

She began to tell everyone around her how much she wanted to play. Her determination quietly grew with each person who said, "Oh, you'd be so good at soccer." And guess who was listening to them, too? Yep, her mom. And at a rather young age, she discovered the power of persuasion—ironically, she would later end up majoring in rhetoric in college.

And within a week, after much persistence, her persuasive skills finally paid off. Her neighbor's soccer team needed another player, and they asked if Little Amy could join their team. Guess who ended up caving to the persuasion? Yep, her mommy.

Amy Sue Agnew, Walnut Creek Quakes soccer team, 1981.

Even though Little Amy had never played soccer before, she certainly wasn't afraid to try. She was ecstatic about learning to play. She was strong, fast, and agile, and discovered that unlike most of the players, she could kick the ball with her left foot! She scored a lot of goals with that left foot. In fact, the next year, she was asked to play on a competitive soccer team.

In the following years, Little Amy played many, many soccer games and scored lots of goals with that left foot... her right foot, too. Adult Amy went on to play many years of coed soccer. And Mommy Amy spent many years coaching her children and countless others on youth-recreation teams. What a difference one yes made.

With her fun and success in soccer, Little Amy jumped at the chance to try more sports.

Her Catholic elementary school, St. Mary's, offered sports in the Catholic Youth Organization (CYO). When she heard about upcoming basketball tryouts, she knew what she wanted to do. The year before, in the third grade, she was a cheerleader for the boys' team. But she spent the whole season wishing she could run out and grab the ball and try to make a basket.

So when tryouts came around in their fourth-grade year, Little Amy and her friends, Jennifer and Pam, decided they would try out for the boys' basketball team. If you can believe it, there weren't any girls' teams in the fourth grade—not until the sixth grade.

There were so many kids trying out that the coaches decided to form three teams. The top boys' players were on the A team. The rest filled the B1 and B2 teams. Not only did the girls make the team, they earned spots on the boys' B1 team. This was 1980—you can imagine the comments and uproar, especially from the B2 team's parents.

Her coach, Mr. Shea, was the father of her classmate and the husband of her fourth-grade teacher. While he was Dad to three boys, he was a champion for his three female players. He never made them feel different or any less capable than the boys on the team.

But at the end of one practice, Little Amy heard her teammate's dad refer to the girls on the team as tomboys. She turned to look at the man, who saw her face, and he quickly turned away. Curious and confused, she wondered, *Tomboy? What does that mean? Pam's older brother is named Tom. But my friends and I definitely aren't boys!*

When she got in the car to leave practice, Little Amy told her mom what the boy's dad said. Her mom frowned and paused before she started the engine of the car. Then, wearing a serious expression, she turned to Little Amy and said defiantly, "That man is a jerk. Just ignore him.

He's just jealous that you girls are better basketball players than his son."

Amy Sue Agnew, Acalanes High School, Lafayette, California, Spring 1982.

With her growing athletic confidence, Tomboy Amy joined her school's CYO track-and-field team. She loved running the individual races and competing in the long jump, but her favorite event was the team relay. Soaring around the track, passing the baton, cheering her teammates to the finish. Tomboy Amy felt unstoppable. And looking at photos of Little Amy on the track, you could almost imagine her Cape flapping strongly behind her.

It's safe to say that Little Amy fell in love with sports—especially the team sports. She loved learning about sportsmanship and being someone other people could count on—both for giving her all on the field, as well as for her kindness and encouragement. She soared in each sport and on every team, and so did the Cape. It kept growing stronger, as she did, and seemed to grow longer as Little Amy grew taller. Wearing her Cape of Capability and Confidence, Little Amy truly felt as if she could do anything.

Yet, over the years, while she appeared confident and fearless on the outside, Little Amy's Cape began to feel a bit heavier. She woke up one day and realized the change in how it felt. Everyone whom she knew seemed to believe "Amy can do anything!" And she often did.

But Little Amy began to worry about a very real future possibility: *What if I can't?*

While Little Amy enjoyed winning races and games, earning ribbons and trophies, success became the expected result of everything she tried. She found herself worrying much more about the outcomes, rather than playing for the joy of the games.

Is the Cape growing heavier with the sticky weight of other people's expectations? What will happen if I don't succeed or win or accomplish things? What if I fail? Who am I really if I'm not performing and succeeding? Will people still like me...love me?

As she grew older, her Cape began to trick her into something called "perfectionism." While playing her beloved sports, Amy discovered a new voice in her mind that didn't feel like her own. No matter how well she played, she wanted more from herself. She criticized the smallest of choices or elements of her performance. She wondered, *If I criticize myself enough, then maybe I won't have to hear it from someone else?* Her attempts began to feel like tests of her capabilities...and she wanted to shine at everything.

Her mean inner voice became even more critical when her dad decided to show up at her games or races. She felt self-doubt and a tentativeness that Little Amy had never known before. She was losing the joy of childhood play. And she was too young to play sports as a job. Sure, she'd love to be a professional athlete someday. But she was just a kid, and she wanted to play like a kid. She wanted to do everything like a little kid...but her world and life circumstances were turning her into a Little Adult Amy way too young.

Chapter 5

The Little Adult

In the years following the divorce, Little Amy's mom—probably grappling with her own disbelief over the change—liked to tell Little Amy that she had been her father's pride and joy. But other than baby photos with him, in which she certainly looked happy and loved, her mother possessed little evidence of Little Amy's past adoring relationship with her father.

Six months after her parents' split—when his divorce from her mommy was final—her dad remarried. And six months after that, her dad and new stepmom drove Little Amy and her brother past a big church in San Francisco. They wanted to show them where they had been married. Little Amy and Randy had not been included in their dad and stepmom's wedding. In fact, they didn't even know it happened until that day in the city when they drove past the big church.

Years later, Young Amy learned that her father had met her stepmom on a plane. She was a stewardess (read, 1970s flight attendant) at the time. He was flying for business and apparently fell in love with the younger woman who had a cute Southern accent and energetic ambition.

Overnight, it seemed, he quickly fell out of love with his "perfect life" at home with his beautiful wife, children, and country club. He wanted "more," and he got what he wanted…for a while.

Little Amy, her mommy, and her brother, however, got far less from his choices. Despite the bitterness her mommy felt towards his new wife (and rightly so), Little Amy found that she reluctantly enjoyed time with her stepmom. And she felt pretty confused and guilty about it.

Like Little Amy, her stepmom was confident, and she had a variety of talents and interests. She too was a dancer and an athlete. She introduced Little Amy to the world of musicals. She represented a different type of 1980s woman than her own mother. But getting to know her stepmom took time, as she very rarely visited her dad's home. And, sadly, when she did, she often felt as if she were a guest visiting for the weekend. In fact, she and her brother didn't even have their own rooms. They slept on the pullout sofa in the upstairs family room. At one point, a dresser was added to the closet. But they weren't allowed to leave clothes or toys in that room. It was the family room, after all.

When Little Amy and Randy were invited to their father's house for a Super Bowl party or holiday, their mom would make bitter comments—for example, "Well, they want to show you guys off to their friends," or, "He only wants to see you when it works best for him."

While those insights were likely spot-on true, they were difficult pills to swallow for a young human. Adult insights are meant for adults, not children who have no control over the situation. Nothing that the children did or felt could, or would, make a difference.

Strangely, the times with their father became unique events to be looked forward to—kind of akin to going on vacation. But they also generated a lot of guilt. Little Amy knew her mommy did all of the real parenting, and she felt guilty having fun with her dad.

When she did get time with her father, it felt as if it was a rapid session of pleasing him. He judged how she played tennis, what clothes she wore (that he never helped buy), what her friends were like. Why wasn't she popular? Why wasn't she just a different daughter?

And when they were out in public with him, she and her brother experienced a constant barrage of him ogling women—"Look at the rack on that one…" "My God, she is beautiful…"—right in front of his children. It would be years before she looked back and realized her father was talking to her and her brother as if they were his buddies instead of his children. Adults shouldn't talk to children that way.

She would be hard-pressed to recall a time when her father showed up in her life with unconditional love. Never did Little Amy hear questions from him similar to "Are you happy? Are you okay? Is there something I can do for you?" Her dad didn't take care of things for her. He asked things of her. Promised he would buy things for her—things she never wanted—on certain conditions.

But when she asked for things of importance to her, like money for field trips or dental insurance, he said he didn't have the money. And yet, just the day before, her stepmom arrived at the tennis court with a brand-new tennis racquet. She and her brother rarely ever felt as if they were priorities at their dad's house.

Little Amy felt that she had to take care of her father's needs in order to feel loved. If she was just smart enough, pretty enough, athletic enough, impressive enough, maybe she would be enough for him. He would want to see her more, cheer her on, support her…just maybe.

The Cape had always been the source of her daring bravery. But as she grew older, wearing the Cape began to feel like a necessity. She needed it to get through life. To achieve so much and so well that her dad would want to see her and spend time with her.

And to do the right thing so as not to disappoint her mom or grandparents. They had never been anything but supportive, yet she wanted to make them happy. And they were happy when she was achieving, winning, and being a hero. So she and the Cape continued their pursuit of pleasing others.

Young Amy was a fun person with an energetic personality. But when it came to trying things that felt wrong, where she might get into trouble (read, disappoint the adults) her Cape said no.

A rule follower, Young Amy wanted to do what was right. The daring little girl with the Cape and "Yes, I can" bravado was slowly disappearing. Her decisions were becoming calculated and measured by the litmus of adult approval. The last thing she wanted to do was get in trouble.

She found a certain comfort in being around adults. They were typically very impressed with her maturity and often called her an "old soul." She loved their attention and approval—it made her feel special and unique. But when it came to friends her own age, she didn't understand why everyone couldn't just be kind and follow the rules.

If one were to spend time with Young Amy's father when she was a teen, they might realize why she had become such a little adult. She was more mature, more adult in her responsible behaviors than he was. She could be counted on to do what she said she would do. She could be relied on—he could not. One might see why she felt the need to always be on guard around him, always uncertain as to what he might do to embarrass and disappoint, or how he might disapprove of her. She was too young to know how to navigate around a narcissist...especially one who happened to be her parent. And no matter how hard she tried, she couldn't get him to show her love or respect.

When she was around her dad, Young Amy did not get to feel like a preteen child. She couldn't focus any carefree energy on the newest Madonna video or whom she was going to the mall with on Saturday. She felt like the adult in their relationship, rather than getting to be a child. She felt responsible for taking care of herself and her brother when they were around their father. She couldn't help but feel more like a Little Adult.

In the spring of 1982, Amy's mom remarried. Dave, a colonel in the army, was a dentist based out of San Antonio, Texas. And, that summer, Amy, her mom, and her brother moved from Northern California to San Antonio, Texas.

Amy's Cape was ecstatic! They had moved before and knew how fun it could be to make new friends, explore new places, new sports teams, new tries. And their new house was not an

Susan, Amy and Randy Agnew, Walnut Creek, California, Spring 1982.

47

attached townhouse. It was a big, sprawling home with a pool! She and her brother felt beyond excited about their new lives and approached the move with optimism and energy.

They attended summer camp at Fort Sam Houston, meeting new kids, swimming, and learning first aid and water rescue. They got to eat in the commissary and spent hours playing Ms. Pac-Man and Donkey Kong at the arcade. They made tons of new friends, swam in their backyard pool, and roller-skated all over the neighborhood. They had the summer of their lives. Little Adult's Cape felt confident, daring, and a bit humid. But, nonetheless, happy.

Until, that is, a few months into their summer, when Texas Amy overheard her mom crying in another room. She was speaking to her best friend in California and talking about "coming home." You see, this plot twist truly seemed to come out of nowhere…and really hurt all three of them.

The dentist had children who were already grown-up and living on their own. And when Young Amy and her brother moved in with him, he apparently decided that he just didn't want to raise two young children again.

We'll let that marinate for a moment…

Needless to say, thriving Texas Amy and her Cape came crashing down to earth. Her mind felt flooded by emotions: rejection, strong urgency to take care of her mother and brother, disappointment at leaving their new life, and apprehension about returning to their old lives. She was afraid, sad, and angry. This solidified, in her young mind, that men could not be trusted or relied upon.

Eleven-year-old Amy became determined in a somewhat-tragic way. When she grew up, she would take care of herself. She would never have to rely on a man. She would earn her education and build a career that afforded financial independence.

She witnessed the impact of this man's selfish decision on her poor mom and her brother. It decimated the last of her carefree, sparkling summer. In those few short months in Texas, her happy childhood self disappeared and was replaced by a determined and protective little adult.

Thankfully, Little Amy's mom had not sold their townhouse in California. She rented it to another family. Her mom's brother, Uncle Grant, flew out to help drive the three of them back to California. And after a month of living in her grandparents' home, they moved back "home" to their townhouse, their Catholic elementary school, and their old lives, as if they had never left.

But they didn't feel normal—not really. The what-ifs of their Texas life would remain in the forefront of their minds. The return left them reeling in shock and uncertainty. It was traumatic.

Sure, California had arcades and a swimming pool, but the scars from the decision her mother was forced to make left Young Amy feeling sheer love and respect for her mom… and disgust towards men. She didn't trust them. But she had a Cape…and she would be her own hero, dammit.

Chapter 6

The Overachiever

After years of being sheltered within the halls of her small Catholic elementary school, Teen Amy made a very adult decision at the end of the seventh grade. She decided to leave the Catholic school system—relieving the tuition burden on her mother—to dive headfirst into the world of public education.

Like most of her thirteen-year-old friends, Teen Amy felt totally awkward. She had never followed a popular music group and had worn a uniform to school most of her life. She felt as if it were totally impossible for her to feel cool: she lacked cool clothing options, she made straight As, she had a relentless feeling of responsibility, and she feared never being enough. And even more uncomfortable was how she felt about her maturing body.

For the first time in her life, body fat began to appear in various awkward places on her body. And, worse, she found she couldn't run as fast as she used to. She felt absolutely confused: she wanted to feel attractive to the boys at school, but she was also very uncomfortable with the idea of looking sexy.

Her discomfort grew, unnecessarily, due to her father's bluntly verbal ogling right in front of her, his constant descriptions of what a beautiful woman should look like, act like. It was incredibly confusing for a young person, let alone for a hormonally maturing young girl. The cringing and discomfort felt constant. Teen Amy increasingly heard, "Boy, your friend Stacey sure is pretty… She looks like a beautiful young woman now!" or other inappropriate comments.

She didn't hear other people's dads talk like that. About how their teenage bodies already looked like women—attractive, tempting. It felt very, very wrong. So why was he doing it? Why was he so different from other dads and uncomfortable to be around? Why did he have to make her feel so uncomfortable and disrespected? Why did he talk to her as if she were a friend? She was his child.

The rocks glass and the Benz

Beautiful women, fancy cars, famous and successful people, Scotch whisky in a rocks glass, and his beloved Mercedes-Benz. This is the short list of things that appeared to dominate her father's mind while other dads were focused on spending time with their children, loving them, taking care of them.

Watching her father hand-wash and wax his 1980 Mercedes-Benz 300D, thistle-green metallic with green MB-Tex upholstery, was akin to observing a stranger. The way he loved that car, spent time with it, cared for it—he reveled in its beauty and the stature it gave him. No person, not even his children, could ever live up to it or be loved by him so unconditionally and generously. He didn't find fault in or criticize the Benz. Just as it was, it was perfect, as was what it gave him. And it was a rare day if he rode in his Benz without a perfectly balanced rocks glass gleaming with a fresh pour of Scotch over ice.

Where did he put the rocks glass? Her memories of riding in that car always contained the sound of the ice clinking in the glass. Back then, cupholders in cars were still a few years away from being a standard item. But her father took great care in assuring that the glass and its liquid remained safe. Just as he did in maintaining a predictable cleanliness and beauty of his car. He expertly perched his rocks glass ever so delicately on the faux-wood center console, just a hand's reach away, next to the radio dial and the air-conditioner controls.

Young Amy couldn't understand why he spent so much time and care on the car and his precious drinks. What did they give him? Why did they make him so happy? Why couldn't he be happy with her and her brother? What did they need to do to take priority over a big green car and a stupid drink on ice?

Being his daughter created such a heavy weight on her heart and soul. Everyone else's fathers were putting them and their needs first, which was what mature adults and parents were supposed to do. But Teen Amy felt the need to make excuses for her dad. Eventually, she got fed up and stopped inviting friends over to his house for sleepovers.

No matter how hard she tried to communicate what she needed from him—using her words to express her feelings in thoughtfully written letters—it never worked. He told her she was nuts, just like her mother. He never took ownership of the toxicity he brought to her life. He never attempted to consider any change in how he showed up for his children.

The more she matured, the less comfortable she felt being around him. And the rocks glass—well, it always made things worse. When the rocks glass was out, she never knew what would come out of her father's mouth. A regular barrage of rude comments, criticism, and condescension rolled off his tongue. The more Teen Amy learned about drugs and alcohol, the more she questioned why her father would choose them over her and her brother.

The adults around her shunned her dad for being "selfish" and "looking out for number one" (himself). According to them, his selfishness caused the pain Teen Amy felt and lived with. So for her, his selfishness became a catalyst for her self-love. She never wanted to be called selfish or self-centered, like her father. He had choices, but made poor ones. She would choose more wisely.

Self-love, self-care, and self-compassion were not common concepts in her family's vocabulary—nor in most American homes during the 1980s. Her Cape of Pleasing was applauded and approved of when it helped Teen Amy become the bearer of generosity and the helper of others, the martyr. Wearing the Cape, Teen Amy found she could be the opposite of what her dad brought to the world. She showed up with selflessness and caring for others and their needs. But, of course, this was at the expense of the child she was.

Being his daughter was disappointing, frustrating, and embarrassing. She spent the rest of her childhood trying her very hardest to be perfect. She went from wearing her Cape to feel happy and fearless, to desperately begging it to help her win, succeed, and please in order to avoid the criticism that made her feel unworthy of love. She couldn't control him, but she sure could control other ways to boost her self-worth. She had a Cape, and she would continue to be her own hero.

Control

Unlike most of her peers, she chose not to drink alcohol or experiment with drugs as a teenager. Teen Amy did not want to lose control of herself the way the rocks glass affected her father and made it even more uncomfortable to be around him.

She figured out that if she kept her mind clear, she could better control the world around her…well, in theory, anyway. She had goals, and she wasn't going to be distracted from achieving them. She felt an interesting sense of control by choosing not to drink alcohol or try drugs. She had suffered firsthand the negative effects of living with an alcoholic.

The one thing she had always been able to control was the magic thread of her Cape: her optimism about life. How did she know her magic was still there? Every time she chose the positive over the negative in life, she felt a surge of energy in her Cape—the gold magic thread lit up all over. People around her couldn't see the gold thread or the Cape, but they could certainly see the magic smile that lit up her face. That surge always reminded Teen Amy that she was in control of her Cape, of the way that she reacted to life, and of the way she focused her Cape. She absolutely was the hero of her story, and no one was going to stop her.

After the eighth grade, Teen Amy soared into the public high school with more social confidence ignited by all of the activities she could try. She knew she wanted to play as many sports as she could. She was the only freshman to make the championship tennis team that year. She thrived on learning and growing with the older girls—she had always wanted an older sibling.

In the winter, she tried out for basketball and made the junior varsity team. At practice one day, her coach described her as tenacious. When she got home that night, she raced upstairs to look up the word in her dictionary. Yes, she definitely was a tenacious person! She loved this new adjective. And she especially loved that her new male coach saw her in that special way.

And then spring came along with a big decision. Should she run track or play softball? Why did they both have to be at the same time? She knew that, logistically, it would be impossible to do both. But she had been running since the third grade, but had not started softball until she was eleven years old.

How can I give up running?

Well, she didn't. Running would go on to be more than just a lifelong exercise. Running activated the magic in her Cape. Made her feel powerful, in control, clear. But, ultimately, she chose to play softball that spring—it was another chance to play as a team with her new friends.

Academically, she found she was near the top of her peers in almost every class. She relished earning a straight-A report card and learned about something called a GPA (grade point average). For this tenacious Cape wearer, it was like the *If You Give a Mouse a Cookie* books. If you give Amy a goal, she'll crush it and ask for more.

If she worked hard academically and earned straight As, she would have a high GPA, and that meant she could get into a great college. And, Teen Amy realized, getting into a great college meant getting a great job and being financially able to take care of herself. Her mother, without a college degree, had struggled to raise two kids on her own; her income potential was limited. So Teen Amy was determined to excel, achieve, get into college, and earn enough money to support herself. She set sail with her Cape towards doing whatever it took for that high GPA.

High school gave her the chance to log countless hours of flying the Cape in several directions at the same time with little sleep, high energy, fierce determination to do it all, and a smile. Most would think it a crazy way to live, but she actually thrived on being that busy. And she lived this busy juggling act for years and years: set a goal, accomplish it, have another on the side, ready to go. She thrived on being busy. She was her own hero, after all.

Amy Sue Agnew, Northgate High School Junior Prom, Walnut Creek, California, Spring 1988.

By the end of freshman year, Teen Amy found that she had friends all over campus. And she quickly developed the nickname Aim, which suited the tenacity of her Cape. She was aiming for the stars.

As much fun as she had at school, Aim was juggling a lot inside her mind. And weekend parties—well, she realized attending those would make her fumble the balls. She didn't want to go to parties, drink, and get into trouble. And when she did go to parties, she felt pressured and questioned about not drinking. All she could think of was the rocks glass and the Benz, and she visualized her college acceptances flying out the window of her dad's car.

Growing Teen Aim and the Cape ran for associated student body vice president at the end of her junior year. The office required her to give an election speech to the entire school, outside on a stage. As she visualized her speech, the Cape strongly flowing behind her, she realized she needed to do something special to stand out and be remembered.

One day, while listening to Ice Cube sing "Straight Outta Compton" (or it might've been Sir Mix-A-Lot's "Posse on Broadway"), she had an idea. Yes, our little adult stretched out of her comfort zone and wrote a rap for her speech. As she nervously delivered the rhymes, Cape flying behind her, she saw the look of utter shock on the kids' faces. No one would've ever imagined that SHE would rap her speech. But she did, and she won the election!

With each try that she successfully achieved, a new layer of capability strengthened the Cape's fabric. And yet, in spite of her achievements, she still felt very much like Little Amy. Everyone, including her, expected Teen Amy to soar at everything she did. And her Cape wasn't immune to the pressure to perform. One day, she discovered in the middle of her Cape a sticky gray goo that felt like her Hubba Bubba Bubble Gum. She pulled the goo off the fabric, wondering how it got there. The gray goo wasn't enough to cause concern or make her doubt her capabilities, though. Once she ignited her magical thread of optimism, the gray tended to disappear.

Until one very sad day when she found the Cape covered in goo. When she started to pull it off, she discovered a very large tear down the middle of the fabric. Pushing her body to try and do it all, she had developed severe tendonitis—a repetitive motion injury—in her right arm.

She was in too much pain—she could barely hold a mug in her hand, let alone a softball bat or a tall flag. It was her last year of high school. She would not heal in time.

The inability to participate in sports made Teen Amy terribly sad, disappointed, and confused. *What kind of Amy will I be if I can't play sports?* She felt a complete loss of identity. She found it extremely difficult to smile, to ignite her magical powers. She sat with her Cape in her hands and cried. For the first time ever, the Cape felt extremely useless, and so did she. Her senior year, the one she had dreamed of—captain of her teams, league MVP dreams, championship runs—would never be realized.

The inability to participate in sports also meant that she'd lost an important tool that kept her Cape healthy. Exercise had always sent magical energy to the Cape. Being connected with her teammates was magical, too. *Who will I be without being a part of a team?* She quickly realized how critical being a member of her team, that tribe of fellow athletes with a common goal, had been to her Cape's success. Without her exercise and organized team activities, she needed to find a replacement source for her magic.

During this plot twist—sports injury—Teen Amy turned to some healthy choices in order to keep the gray off her growing Cape. After   writing down her feelings and talking to friends, she remembered that she was more than just an athlete. The tomboy was also a dancer, a student, a leader, and a courageous Cape wearer.

Plot Twist

Realizing the need to visualize a different senior year of high school, Teen Amy began to imagine herself healing from her injury and returning to her athletic life. She wondered what would happen if she put the same effort into healing as she had into playing. Perhaps she could be even stronger than before the injury. Her what-if mindset returned.

She accepted the loss of her sports and channeled the magic into her resilience to try new things her last year of high school. She applied for a job at a yogurt shop, earned spending money, and for the first time, had time to simply hang out with friends after school.

Before long, resilience could once again be seen strengthening the edges of her Cape. Even better, Amy learned that people liked her for who she was, not just what she accomplished on the court or the field.

And yes, those big envelopes carrying college acceptances did fill her mailbox. In the end, she chose the college and town she had spent a lot of time in during her senior year, visiting her older best friend. And while it was the cheapest option, and the college closest to home, more importantly, it was the environment in which she knew she could be her most authentic self.

With diploma in hand, High School Grad Amy soared into her first summer of young adulting. Wrapping up the season of Little Amy, she began to prepare for the first episode of a new season of her life. Little Amy had achieved her primary goal—she was going to college. Everything that she had worked for, all of the effort and sacrifice, had paid off. It was time to dream new dreams and become whoever she wanted to be.

Daring Little Amy took the front seat on the Cape. She challenged herself to let her Cape fly for the fun in life. To live a little, take chances, and start anew. She felt determined to leave Little Amy behind and see what Young Adult Amy was capable of. And the possibilities felt limitless—she had a Cape with superpowers, after all.

Part 2 ~ Early Adulting

Chapter 7

Sorority Aim

It was the fall of 1989, Amy's version. Janet Jackson's *Rhythm Nation* blared on high volume from the headphones attached to her portable CD player. The pushpin on the sign on her dorm-room door stated that she was, "Out on a Run!" Sorority T-shirt, shorts, and megawatt smile, her Cape flapping happily behind her, College Aim ran to stay in shape, to work through her stress, and—well, if we're honest—to check out the fraternity guys hanging out in front of their houses.

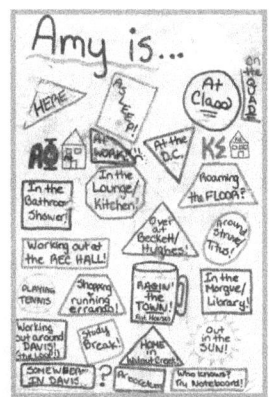

Sign on the outside of Amy Agnew's dorm room, University of California Davis, Davis, California, 1989.

From the moment she landed on campus, College Amy's Cape could not be contained. She bounded into her sorority-rush dorm room and started to fly. She refused to let Little Amy step foot into her college world. She was on fire and ready to live her best life. And she was going to let nothing stop her.

Her magic thread of optimism radiated across the Cape, ablaze with excitement, craving adventure and endless possibilities. It was likely the closest she had felt to utter joy and total fearlessness since the day she first discovered her Cape. She was free to be whichever Amy she wanted to be. The responsible, goody-goody girl was hopefully on a very long hiatus.

Now, before we get too crazy, let's remember that the little adult was still inside of Amy and well embedded in the foundational layer of the Cape. Her idea of going crazy and living in a carefree manner was considerably tamer than those of most of her newly minted freshmen friends. But the day her mother and brother dropped her off in the dorms, she couldn't get them to leave fast enough. She was ready to live and experience college life to the fullest.

Just two weeks before the start of her freshman year, she participated in sorority rush (nowadays known as sorority recruitment). Her best friend from high school had been a freshman at the same university the year before and had pledged a sorority. Teen Amy spent lots of time visiting her friend during her own senior year of high school, so she had a taste of what life could be like in her new college town. She knew that rushing a sorority would be a great way to meet people before school started. But she just wasn't sure she would be able to pick just one house to commit to.

This was, after all, the girl who played multiple sports and engaged in many activities in high school. She didn't want to be labeled as one thing over another. At this time in her life, she wanted to experience all that the world could offer, to live in the now, and to let nothing hold her back.

Although she felt confident and capable of shining, she naturally also worried about how she would be perceived during sorority rush. Would the girls like her? Would the right houses want her? Did she even know what would be the right house for her? And what if that changed over time? All valid concerns, but she certainly didn't let them stop her.

The Cape itself was ready to let go of the heavy responsibility that had dominated Amy's actions for so many years. Any fear that creeped in was completely snuffed out by the magic threads' energy, excitement, and wonder. The Cape was ready to TRY and live. And so was College Amy.

Given the title of this chapter, you, the reader, can correctly assume that College Amy did indeed pledge a sorority. In fact, she was fortunate to have her pick of houses. And in the end, she chose a sorority filled with girls who enjoyed the wide range of interests that she did.

During rush, she met different types of new friends who would bring out the many different sides of College Amy. She knew she could show up as herself in this house, and she would also be encouraged to grow. The older sorority sisters felt as if they were the big sisters she never had. They made her feel young, carefree, and cared for. Little Amy felt so supported.

How could she have realized the impact that her choice in sorority would end up having on her life? Such a huge pivotal moment yielded lifelong connections. Many of those young girls would become dear old friends and occupy front-row seats to view College Amy's journey into adulthood.

This Phi on Fire, or the Super Pledge, lived her absolute best life

Amy Agnew, Alpha Phi Sorority house, UC Davis, Davis, California, 1993.

during her four years of college, in spite of quite a few very difficult circumstances. This college chapter likely deserves its own book, or perhaps a Netflix miniseries. But the most important things to know about Sorority Aim?

- Academics were not the priority for the first time in her life. She had proven she could crush a GPA. But she was a solid-B student in college. Letting herself have fun, building relationships, and learning life skills took priority.
- She had to pay for college and received little financial aid. There was no FAFSA back then. And, if you can imagine, they counted her single mom's equity in her home against her (yes, the value of her home if she sold it). She worked countless different jobs—a nanny, a coffee barista, a yogurt-shop clerk, a manager of personal ads for the campus newspaper—and she even took Classical Notes for the classes she attended.

Amy Agnew with Alison, Emily & Matthew Arkfeld, Davis, California, 1993.

- She had a LOT of fun. She was a sorority girl, after all. Eventually, and reluctantly, she learned to like the taste of beer—even learned how to crush a keg stand. She played multiple intramural sports and often enjoyed playing on many different teams each quarter. She had never had so much fun in her life, nor felt so carefree and happy.

- On top of her academic workload, sorority commitments, and busy social life, at the same time, she lived a double life, struggling through many very adult difficult experiences.
    - For financial independence, she worked full time every summer to save for her tuition. But she was never really sure if she'd have enough money to stay in school and pay for living expenses each quarter. And then there were her dad's bounced checks and stretching twenty-five dollars to buy groceries each week. She became extremely resourceful and savvy about money, both earning and spending it. The majority of her friends had no idea what she was shouldering and how much pressure it put on top of everything else she was trying to do…every…single…day.
    - At twenty-one, she endured major jaw surgery and wore braces for two years of college. She battled a great deal of constant jaw pain.
    - Thanks to her dad's poor decisions, she fought the IRS for her mom. They won, but too late to help her qualify for financial aid for college.
    - And then there was the night she had too much to drink and called a friend to take her home from a frat party. Turns out, he wasn't such a good friend, after all.

Daily, it was impossible for College Amy to avoid feeling a tremendous amount of stress. But Sorority Aim just kept smiling through it. She was determined to make the most of every moment. And what about the Cape? Well, it spent every day of college deflecting doubt, disappointment, and fear, and becoming an expert at producing the Amy Smile.

Some chapters from the *Book of Sorority Aim* might include: "Struve 2 TOC" (dorm floor, totally out of control); "Phi Pledge Class"; "The College Apartment Pool Scene"; "Theme Dances, Mono, and the Gulf War"; "TGs, Formals, and Campus Candid Photos"; "Adult Braces and Jaw Surgery"; "The Men—The Good, the Bad, and the Awful"; "Running, Blading, and Intramurals"; "Starving Student, Loser Dad, and the Bounced Checks."

Accomplishments crushed and life skills built: college degree; solid work resume; Greek Week director; commencement speaker runner-up; Sorority Woman of the Year; lifelong friendships; expansive network; life savvy, capability, and responsibility; fearlessness.

What did the Cape gain? More heavy layers of ambition, people pleasing, and perfectionism; depression and hiding of the gray layer; more distrust of men; several fresh layers of survival; a relentless resilience. Neither the Cape nor College Amy let anything stop them—they just kept pushing through. Isn't that what superheroes do?

College Aim and the Cape successfully navigated their way to a college degree. They did it! And like most of her peers, College Grad Amy was kept up at night with the looming question, *Now, what am I going to do?*

For the first time in her life, she wasn't sure. Which way should she go? She could try her hand in the corporate world, or she could go on to graduate school and become a professor.

She turned twenty-two years old the same weekend she graduated and began preparing to backpack through Europe for the first time. Four weeks of exploring the world, staying in hostels, meeting people, and finding someone to practice her high school Spanish with. Her career plans would have to wait.

Amy Agnew, UC Davis Graduation, Davis, California, June 1993.

For graduation, her grandparents gifted her Dr. Seuss's *Oh, the Places You'll Go!* The words became her inner mantra.

Chapter 8

London Calling

Bachelor's degree in hand, Graduate Aim and her college best friend embarked on a four-week journey backpacking through Europe. After nearly twenty-four hours of plane travel, they landed in Nice, France—dropping onto a landing strip right on the water. Exhausted, excited, and terrified, she realized she had landed in a world where she had no idea how to communicate with anyone. The situation felt both terrifying and amazing!

From the moment she stepped off the plane and waited for her luggage in Baggage Claim, she knew her life was changing forever. She could feel the magic activating her Cape. There really was a big, big world waiting for her, and this was just the beginning of her life of travel.

She discovered that she absolutely loved everything about traveling: meeting new people, exploring new places, seeing in real life places she had studied, and trying everything and anything new. Her travels planted the seed to return to Europe someday…and possibly live abroad. While she hadn't been able to afford to study abroad as an undergrad, her four weeks in Europe ignited her adventure magic in a way she couldn't quite describe. She visualized that seed of an idea and resolved to make it happen someday.

Upon returning to the States, Adventure Amy chose to attend graduate school for communications at her undergraduate university. She kept picturing herself lecturing at one of the finest universities in the world. *Can it happen? Why not?*

The best part of her choice in graduate school choice? Well, there were two. First, it allowed her another year with all of her college friends who were in their fifth year of undergrad. *Why did I rush to graduate in four years?* She really wasn't ready to leave her friends or the "safety" of college life. Now, she didn't have to.

Second, the decision confirmed just how much she loved to teach. As a graduate student, she taught undergraduate communication courses—small group dynamics and public speaking. Teaching and facilitating discussions came naturally to her, and they filled her with so much joy. She knew she had uncovered a big natural skill. She was absolutely authentically herself when she taught. But, sadly, her graduate program and courses did not bring the same happiness.

After a year of graduate school, Instructor Amy knew that the graduate program at her university was not the right fit for her. She hated to quit anything, but her instincts told her that her environment was not the right one for her. She felt it in her gut. She had learned to trust her gut. And while she felt afraid to leave the program, she knew that this path was not the right one. Something needed to change.

She didn't know what she would do next for work or school, but she happened to know where she wanted to go. Lingering in her university's travel office one day, she discovered a British/North America work-exchange program. Since she was still within six months of being a student, she qualified for a work visa to live and work abroad.

The Cape began to glow. She had found a way. She could do this. She could really make her dream of living in Europe come true!

Well, you can probably guess what happened next. With the same excitement and determination that she felt when starting college, Grad Student Amy had a new goal, and she made a plan. She moved home for a few months to live with her mom and save money. She found office work through a temporary agency and calculated how long she needed to work to save for her adventure abroad.

And in October of 1994, Newly Minted Adult Amy boarded a plane to London—long wool coat and two very large suitcases in hand. As she waved goodbye to her family and boyfriend, the Cape unfurled itself yet again, and she found herself feeling utterly fearless. The world was waiting for her, and she was on her way!

Now, you can probably imagine the adventures that a twenty-three-year-old young woman might have living in London. Especially one with a capable Cape and a fierce de-

Amy Agnew, London, England, January 1995.

sire to live her best life. But you'll just have to keep imagining since—besides a few photos—there is no actual proof of what happened...

Remember, in 1994, electronic mail (read, email) was new to the world, and it wasn't very user-friendly. In fact, only some nerdy college people seemed to be giving it a test-drive. For the technology savvy few at the time, there were internet cafes in Europe. (Yes, places where you could buy time on a desktop computer to access the internet to send an email.)

And get this—there were no cell phones. No cameras on a cell phone. No texting or apps (applications), no social media, no digital tools. That's right. No instant text messaging, selfies, Facebook, Twitter, Instagram, or TikTok to document every experience she had with people from all over the world.

In fact, if she wanted to capture a photo from one of her many weekend adventures throughout Great Britain, or even just a fun evening at the pub, it was a bit of a production. She had to pull the camera out of her bag, put film in the camera, snap photos until all the film was used, and then have the film developed at a photo lab of some sort. It was there that she would pay for the prints, sort through them, and then throw the bad shots into a trash can. Personal cameras in the 1990s were just not very good.

And if there were any appropriate prints (read, post worthy) for Mom, she stuffed the decent ones into an envelope, delivered the package to a post office, purchased international air-mail postage (*par avion*), and mailed them to her mother. If she was lucky, there was a solid chance that her mom would receive the envelope with said photos before Amy returned from her adventure...months later.

And if she wanted to actually speak with her family back in the States, she had to use something called a calling card (read, credit card for a phone call). She took her MCI calling card and looked for a red British phone booth—they were everywhere—that was not occupied. Her mom, brother, or grandparents would have to accept the call before they could be connected, and then they raced through what they had to say because every single minute was a hefty financial investment. The calls were very brief, but in the mid-1990s, they were her mom's only "proof of life" for her globe-trotting twenty-three-year-old daughter. Period.

Living in London was as amazing as it might sound. For the first time in her life, she made decisions all by herself—it was too expensive to ask her mom. She was able to really listen to her gut: *What feels right to me, right here and now?* Not what she thought she should do, or what the mom-approved choice might be.

But as any older adult knows, young adults don't always make the best gut-based decisions…and that's how they learn. And London Aim learned a lot.

Between college and this time living abroad, the Cape had grown longer and leaner, quickly jettisoning her into adulthood…and the training wheels were off. She made a few mistakes. But she always looked for the valuable lessons and turned lemons into lemonade. And, boy, did she have some amazing stories to share when she got home.

And the Cape? Well, it loved Amy's independence and carefree perspective. It lost count of Amy's many tries. It felt euphoric—as if it could carry Amy anywhere to do anything.

And by early 1995, she found herself with a permanent job offer, a really cute Aussie boyfriend, and a growing love for London—this place she called home for a truly lovely chapter of her life. It was the dead of winter. She spent her first Thanksgiving and Christmas away from home. In fact, she spent Christmas in a castle and New Year's Eve in Scotland for Hogmanay! But those stories are surely for another time.

Might she have stayed in London if it were 2024—instead of 1994—with all the instant communication and connection with her family and friends that technology would offer? Perhaps. During this time of her life, the magic of the Cape felt limitless. She could visualize taking on the world—maybe she'd build a career as a diplomat or even an ambassador.

London Amy could visualize putting down her roots and building her life there. It was easy to imagine. But in the midst of her ambition and visualization, her heart tugged hard to the ends of her Cape. She also very much missed her family and friends. Her best friend's nineteen-year-old brother had died tragically in an accident before she left. Her own grandmother was having health issues. She was worried about the people she loved, and she wanted to share her life with them.

After months of working as a secretary—an administrative assistant—she was bored. She was ready to start her "real" career. She wanted to continue her studies and finish graduate school. She easily imagined herself teaching at a university. Perhaps return to Britain to teach someday? But for now, she needed to come back down to earth and begin building her adult life back home in California. And so she said, "So long, London."

What would she carry with her from this dreamy life chapter?

- Regardless of which chapter of Amy's life she lived, she authentically loved meeting new people. Congeniality seemed to be one of the Cape's gifts.
- She built the confidence that she could do any job she put her mind to, including lunch-order taker, tea maker, receptionist, executive secretary, computer support technician, all-things-American expert…
- British men can be handsome, and their accents are dreamy…but their personalities can be very boring.
- Aussies and Kiwis are very much like Californians (read, fun)…and *not* boring.
- A student-concession discount could give you access to the cheapest experiences in 1995 Europe:
    - The most remarkable West End show seats (front row) for about five quid (read, five dollars)—she saw twelve shows during her time there.
    - Access to the Guinness Brewery tour and two fresh pints of deliciousness could be enjoyed for one quid (read, one British pound or one dollar).
    - The British Railway pass transported her all over the United Kingdom. Their railway system is a true marvel—America missed an opportunity for efficient travel.
- The Museum of Everyday Things in York, England, was one of the coolest museums she ever experienced.

- London nightclubs in the mid-1990s were truly epic. That is all.
- Spending New Year's Eve in Edinburgh, Scotland, for three days of Hogmanay, should be on everyone's bucket list...especially twenty-somethings.
- Amy, no matter her age, will forever be drawn to all things British—except the food. Well, maybe fish-and-chips—they are delicious, but not for every meal.

Living in London truly felt like a dream. And in some ways, it really was one. But globally influenced Aim was ready to dive into some real adulting. After an exceptional all-night do (read, party) with all of her London mates, she reluctantly boarded a Virgin Atlantic airplane. As the plane lifted off, and the reality of leaving her London life set in, the fabric of responsibility seemed to come right back to the forefront of her Cape.

Getting off the plane in San Francisco, she experienced a solid dose of culture shock. She'd forgotten what sunglasses were for. She would forever call the restroom the loo. And she knew that memories or references to London would always and forever activate a special magic in her Cape.

Chapter 9

Twenty-Something

This quarter-life period of Amy's life is a great time to take a little pause…to remember there is no playbook or instruction manual for becoming an adult. To reflect on how far and long Little Amy and her Cape navigated without any…as a child, a little adult, and a young adult.

In our journey to find Little Amy, we needed to revisit her youth to understand where the Cape came from and to observe how Little Amy navigated life with her Cape. She was a naturally happy person, preferring to smile, instead of feel sad, and to help others while achieving her own goals. But she felt she could never ask for help while shouldering the burden of the growing Cape. Taking off the Cape or showing any vulnerability would ruin the superhero persona she was determined to maintain.

She kept pushing the Cape to its limits, but there were few limits to her imagination. She dreamed and lived big while managing the gray stickiness that often attached itself to the Cape's fabric and threatened her way of life. To live as the hero of her own story meant keeping the superhuman Cape on tight, no matter the cost.

At the same time, she loved to learn and wanted to become a better version of herself. It was that desire and her persistence that allowed her to grow. To learn to listen to her intuition and weigh her gut feelings against the preferences of others.

Over the years, people challenged her ideas, yet she held firm when she felt deep in her gut that she had the right idea. And her confidence grew. She learned to trust herself. Retain her optimism. Be authentically Amy.

Upon returning from London, she followed her heart and figured out how to go back to college to finish her graduate degree and ultimately teach college communication. Her intuition about there being a better graduate program for her was right. The new university's program fit her to a tee, and she loved her experience. She was even awarded Graduate Student of the Year! Her rekindled passion for academics led her to apply to and be accepted for PhD programs—she wanted to be a college professor.

Amy Agnew, California State University East Bay, Hayward, California, June 1996.

Graduate degree in hand, Masters Amy had never felt more fearless and inspired. One might believe that she and her Cape had hit their prime. She could clearly visualize the next four years of her life. Studying and teaching in a PhD program, single, and fancy-free. Nothing could stop her or get in the way of the life she had so clearly imagined. There were no longer any forks in the road!

But during that summer of 1996, two pivotal events and a chance meeting triggered a new trajectory for Amy's second quarter of life, all while waiting for PhD program acceptances. First, she traveled to Europe with her mom and brother. She returned feeling even more like an adult, more confident that the world was her oyster. Second, she met her future husband at a Taco Tuesday event in her hometown. Then, she was offered her first professional job—working for a brilliant woman in a company's training department.

Suddenly, before she could even process these changes, the idea of four more years of college didn't seem so appealing. Amy had discovered a whole new oyster. *How could I have anticipated this fork in the road or these exciting new options that life brought?*

Unlike the scary plot twists in her life, these pivotal quarter-life moments brought her exciting choices. And she knew the choices were hers—which was thrilling and scary, all at once. *How could I have imagined two totally different life paths, both of which have the potential to make me happy? How do I choose one over the other?*

She knew that the answer lay in the power of those questions. She needed to imagine what lay on each path beyond the fork in the road. Since that day in the townhouse—when she learned of her parents' divorce—she had been developing a superpower that helped her face decisions head-on.

Her response to indecision was to visualize what life would look and feel like on each potential path. As a perfectionist, she was certainly afraid to make the wrong decision. But she overcame her fears by considering what would make her feel like her truest self. And by reminding herself that she could always switch gears and try the other path someday, as she did when she went back to school to earn her PhD.

In the midst of this major pivotal moment in life, she followed the path that caused a magical glow to wash over her Cape. She chose the unexpected path—the professional career. She found herself living with energy, hope, and positivity. She was in love. And she was falling in love with this unexpected path.

She had spent the past six years working and going to college and graduate school. The idea of earning a great salary and having nights and evenings free to be a carefree twenty-something, well, it was just too exciting to turn down. And so, once again, she trusted her gut to make the very best of this new chapter.

She found herself happily immersed in the exciting life of a young working professional. She and her boyfriend rented a house with a big backyard. Which meant she could finally adopt a dog, who became affectionately known as her first child. And she enjoyed a real, solid income for the first time ever. She even started to build a savings account.

And in those next four years, rather than study to earn her PhD, Twenty-Something Amy built a life down the chosen fork. She jumped into her career and went on to marry the guy, move to her old college town to buy a house, and begin raising a family.

But let's put the car in reverse a bit... About a year into her decision to turn away from the PhD path and to accept the professional job, she made another very mature, adult decision. You can imagine how many things Amy's mind had processed and attempted to piece together over the nearly twenty years since her seventh birthday. In spite of her relentless optimism, she couldn't help but feel frustrated by the growing stickiness and heaviness of the Cape. She knew she was afraid to trust her new romantic relationship. She had struggled to trust men for as long as she could remember. And she felt confused about juggling her dreams and those of someone else. She was tired of running away from love, but didn't know how to manage her fears.

Of course, she felt all those things—she lacked a healthy role model. If she was going to be the hero of this new chapter of her story, she needed help. Her Cape was still light enough that she could recognize when something new was added to weigh her down. She decided to learn how to stop running from her fears. And she knew that choice likely meant processing her trauma, disappointments, and emotions. Asking for help seemed as if it was the smart thing to do for a girl determined to soar with a Cape.

For the first time in her twenty-six years, she made the choice to see a therapist. She had questions that needed answers, including *What is the gray stickiness that keeps appearing on my Cape and weighing it down when I feel happy and excited about life? How can I remove it?* She had benefited from so many sports coaches over the course of her life; why wouldn't a mind coach help?

In the first session with Dr. Solomon, she knew she had made the right decision. Together, they found the root of so much of her fear and pain. He validated the trauma that she had experienced. He commended her for still finding a way to fly with her Cape, as tattered as it had often felt. He was the first person to say out loud to her, "Your father is supposed to take care of you, his child." She, of course, had always known that deep down. Yet the validation from a stranger was, well, very helpful. And she sighed, almost out of relief.

Her determination and decision to get help and begin processing the weight of the past was a critical pivotal moment in her young adulting life. She knew that she wanted to feel more free and less afraid when it came to men and relationships. And she was very, very tired of overachieving.

But as anyone who has started therapy for the first time knows, she had only just opened Pandora's Box—the processing work had only just begun. Processing, healing, and accepting would be a very, very long way off. Yet she was learning and willing to do the work—even though the feelings were really hard to process.

Early Adulting Amy began to address some of the deepest pain from her past that had been hidden deep in her heart and mind. The process made her feel enlightened and hopeful. She wanted to eventually get married and build a family. But she was determined to raise children who felt differently than she while growing up.

The last thing that she wanted was for her marriage to end in divorce and for her kids to have to endure a split family. That idea alone forced her to build walls between men and her. In her dream future, Adult Amy's children would never have to worry about pleasing parents who were at odds with one another. They wouldn't have to question their parents' priorities or determine under what conditions they would be loved and feel safe. They would feel unconditional love and never have to question their worth or their parents' pride.

She imagined a life in which her children's use of their Capes could be focused solely on channeling the courage to do and try all that they wanted to try in this life—instead of for escape and survival. *Can't I parent so well that I am able to shield my children from the serious disappointments, traumas, and fear that life brings?* With that whole illusion of having control over her children's lives, her mind coach certainly had his work cut out for him. Sure, she knew that pain was a part of life. But for her children, she was determined to do her best to create an environment that fostered healthy minds and hearts.

How will this newly recovering perfectionist navigate the temptations of having it all? How can I avoid thinking I have to be exceptional at everything I attempt, balance, juggle, all at the same time? While I want to raise healthy-minded children, can I myself learn how to keep my own Cape healthy?

Amy likely saw these questions as a worthy challenge—something she could strive to accomplish, but of course not over-accomplish. At twenty-something, Amy was beginning to understand the duality of her Cape. She felt great confidence in her capabilities, but also her resolve was softened by her mortal limitations. She felt a strong desire to control the world around her. Her expectations grew larger, both for others and herself.

As she navigated the future chapters of her life, mind coaches would come and go. During the gap years, who would remind her that while she was a wonder of a woman, she was not actually superhuman?

Chapter 10

And What Do You Do?

Some people grow up wanting to follow in their parents' footsteps. But Little Amy didn't really have a career role model in her mom or dad—she couldn't relate, ambitionwise, to either of them.

While her dad was very successful when she was younger, his desire for more led him down a very unhealthy road. He was far from a source of stability or sage advice about careers or life. He was chasing money and fame, and couldn't be bothered to pay her dental bill.

And for as long as she could remember, she struggled to relate to her mother's desire to be nothing more than a mom. While she dearly loved and respected her mom, and was so grateful for all that she did for her and her brother, she felt as if her mom just couldn't relate to her.

In her twenties, her mom won runner-up in the Miss Oakland pageant. The world was a very different place then. In the 1960s, girls were not typically encouraged to be independent or to have careers. Beauty pageants, however, were to be celebrated. Amy's mother was beautiful, tiny, and petite. Amy always hoped she'd grow up to be just like her, but petite she would never be. Tall, strong, and athletic were her genetic cards.

Amy was driven by ambition and possibility, while her mother was raised to be afraid to dream, was told that she was "too" something to try anything. Thankfully, Amy's mom didn't want her own kids to experience the doubt and insecurities that she had felt growing up. And so, as you'll recall from the early stories of Little Amy, she encouraged Amy and her brother to try most things.

So, yes, when she imagined herself as a mother, Amy absolutely wanted to be as loving and committed as her mother had always been for her. But as far as "just" being a mom, well, Amy had always felt flabbergasted by that idea. For as long as she could recall, she couldn't imagine why "being a mom" was all that her mom would ever aspire to be. *Doesn't she know there is a whole world of experiences out there to live?*

Younger Amy vehemently wanted to *be* so much more. After all, women had been fighting for decades to give her generation of women the chance to be more than unappreciated, powerless, domestic people—"*just* moms."

And her ambitious desires drove Amy to dare to dream of doing amazing things with her life: a professional tennis player, a diplomat, a sportscaster, a doctor… Because being "just a mom" felt like the opposite extreme of her dream. It felt like a sacrifice. She had watched her mom sacrifice everything for Randy and her; Twenty-Something Amy did not want to repeat that pattern and lose herself. At least, that is how it felt at the time.

And so, after finishing graduate school and choosing to reject the PhD path, she began her professional career. She didn't know where it was going to lead, but she was learning, growing, demonstrating her capabilities, and earning a paycheck. And her Cape glowed as it rested over her beautiful blazers.

Professional Amy found success in the world of learning and development—it allowed her to tap into her strengths as a teacher while still earning a large corporate paycheck. She had always loved designing learning experiences, and now found it was fun to teach adults, too. It required all of her strengths, and she felt as if the possibilities for her professional career were limitless. How could she have ever imagined, at that time, that being a mom would be the most amazing job she would ever have?

Baby Emily was born in the middle of the night on a rainy autumn morning. With both parents half asleep and the hospital quiet, except for the beeps of the vital-signs monitor, they stared at their newborn baby. Wide-eyed, Emily stared back at her mom's face. Her own surprise and wonder seemed to mirror her mother's.

In the moments Emily entered the world, Mommy Amy was born too. And staring at her perfect little miracle, suddenly nothing else mattered. She would protect this baby with her life.

Now, those early months of life with a newborn are times that no one can truly prepare you for. Some parents luck out with babies who are good sleepers. Mommy Amy and her husband? Well, they did not. Weeks upon weeks of issues with breastfeeding, colic, sleeplessness, illnesses... If you know, you know. It was brutal.

One awful night in particular, during a shift change at 3:00 a.m., Mommy Amy's husband proclaimed, "Why are there so many people in this world? Don't people remember this??"

By three months in (it's hard to remember specifically), things began to level out. Sleep returned, as did some of Amy's brain. Her colleagues began asking when they could expect her back on the job. Working from home was very, very, very unusual in the year 2001, but her tech company was on the cutting edge of corporate cultures. She had worked remotely right up to Emily's birth and hoped to continue. But she expected that her evolving role would require weekly time in the office.

Mommy Amy was growing tired of the Groundhog Day cycle of her life and of feeling like a cow (yes, she was breastfeeding). It was time to figure out her next steps. She needed to return to her corporate professional self. Right? That's what she had worked for all of these years. She was a mom *and* a professional. *Why can't I do both? Isn't that what my modern elders fought for?*

Yet, the day before she was set to return to work, commuting ninety minutes down to the office, she found herself staring in the mirror. Naturally, she felt scared. And she was flooded by uncertainty and doubt. *Am I really ready? Can I make this work? What is best for my daughter? My team? My family? Me?* The only way to find out was to try. And that made her remember her Cape. She would find a way...

So she engineered a masterful return-to-work plan, taking advantage of her company's unique telecommuting option to get herself back into the office. Her mom and grandmother still lived in the East Bay, which gave her (and Emily) a place to stay one night a week. Her leader approved her plan to work remotely three days a week and travel to the East Bay for two days a week in office. Since Amy's mom worked full time, too, the plan was for

Amy and Baby Emily to travel to Amy's grandma's house early in the morning on day one, drop Emily off, and then drive the nineteen remaining miles to her office.

Emily would stay with her GG (great-grandma) until Grandma Sue picked her up in the afternoon after she got off work. After Amy finished working with her team at the office, she would drive to their mother's house and spend the night. The next morning, she would drop Emily off at GG's and then drive to the office. After leaving the office that night, she would pick up Emily and drive back to their home, an hour away.

They would do this every week. Sounds like a great plan, right? Amy was determined to make it work. She wore a Cape. Of course, she could have it all!

Amy loved her job, her team, and wanted to find a way to have it all. Her team was a group of intelligent, wonderful coworkers whom she had happily onboarded and coached. They were all thriving together, and it made her so happy. She was proud of what they had all accomplished together.

But this arrangement was absolutely taking a toll on Amy. While there were several positives to the juggle—including a good income, medical benefits, and weekly time with the four generations of women—Amy felt splintered between two different lives.

A month into the execution of her masterful plan, one sunny afternoon at her team's weekly staff meeting, another pivotal life event occurred. Her mind had been struggling to manage everything for months. Daydreaming, she looked out the window, and her mind drifted. She wondered what Emily was doing. *I know she is in great hands with her own grandma. But what am I, Mommy Amy, missing? Did Emily do something new?*

Then, mirrored in the window, she caught her own reflection…and a glimpse of her Cape. She was shocked to see it still on her back. *Has it been there all these months, underneath my blazer while I drive around trying to make everything happen? Can I see it now because it is time to make another big decision? But how can I just walk away from the career I have built?*

She couldn't work part-time in her current role, and she was tired of being a full-time employee with very little left to give her role as Mom. It was at that moment that she realized she did not want to live the juggling act anymore.

Seeing her Cape in the reflection made her feel strong, just as Little Amy used to feel. And so she began to imagine her two different options: continue with the current plan, or stop the madness and find another. This visualization process, as usual, revealed what felt best to her heart and her Cape. She knew she could find other ways to contribute to the family income. She would find another way to keep her professional brain and skills fresh. She and the Cape had always found a way.

And so she chose her daughter…and, equally, the job she never imagined would bring her such joy. She chose motherhood as her primary job. She didn't want someone else raising her child or experiencing all of her firsts. She chose for Emily, but also for her.

And she chose to take off the heavy weight of having to do it all. While she was really afraid to walk away from her career for the time being, she knew in her gut it was what she wanted right then and there.

The future? Well, she'd figure that out as she went. For now, being a mom was the role that felt most important to her. And yes, her own mother smiled—she loved this decision.

If asked, "And what do you do?" Mommy Amy replied, "I'm a stay-at-home mom." But, of course, she was never "just" a mom and rarely ever stayed at home! What a silly name for such an incredible role! Her Cape was still on, and she was determined to be so much more than what she had always deemed a sacrifice. While she relished the challenges of this new chapter of life, she would certainly be more than "just" anything.

And a few years later, on a rainy, late-summer morning, Emily's little brother entered the world. The pregnancy had been an incredibly challenging one, both physically and mentally. He had been a twin, whom Amy had lost at around fourteen weeks, so this healthy baby boy felt like a miracle to her. She had lived with so much fear throughout her pregnancy, wondering if he would make it. And now she could take a deep breath.

As she held both of her babies close, Mommy Amy felt utterly complete. There was absolutely no doubt in her mind that what mattered most in her world were the two little people she held in her arms. The two little people whose lives she was already dreaming about. And she would protect them with her life...and her Cape.

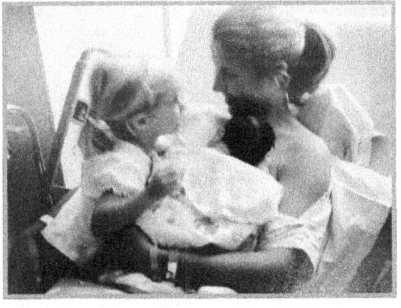

Amy, Emily & Colby Irvine, Sacramento, California, July 2003.

Chapter 11

Super Mommy

Before we dive into the life of Super Mommy, it's important to understand Amy's state of mind heading into motherhood. After working with her mind coach, Adult Amy actively practiced strategies to help manage her overachiever tendencies. It was a hard, slow, often-frustrating process. And her return to her professional life had certainly tested her.

As Amy examined her own behaviors and reactions to life, and the very mean way she spoke to herself, she felt rather raw. *How would I feel if my children treated themselves in the same way? Spoke so meanly to themselves? Do I want my children to push themselves so hard for reasons that have nothing to do with their own satisfaction? To drive themselves with such a relentless pace? To put others' needs consistently over their own? Of course not.*

By the time her children came along, Mommy

Matt, Amy, Emily & Colby Irvine, Davis, California, October 2003.

95

Amy was determined and intentional about not wanting to raise perfectionists. In fact, when her second child was born, she looked at her own mother and said, "I don't care what they do for work or whom they love, I just want to raise emotionally happy and healthy people." Her mother thought the epidural had caused Amy to go a little wacky. But no. She was determined to raise children who felt unconditionally loved. No matter what, she would love them and raise them with confidence and capability, without the heavy weight of pleasing others.

As noble and lovely as these goals sound, Momma Amy forgot that she was not actually a superhero. She was living in the early stages of recovery from being an overachiever. No matter her intentions, her mindset and behaviors couldn't just change overnight. Perfectionism would likely continue to challenge her for the rest of her life.

And raising her kids in a culture of success? Well, she would only be able to do so much. She wouldn't always be there to help her children process the world. Once they got into school, they had to learn how to ingest and decipher what the world gave them. Life has a way of happening, despite our best intentions. All she could control was how she modeled kindness to others and herself. And she had no idea how much resilience and courage she would end up demonstrating and being the role model for in the years to come.

In those early years of raising little ones, life without a career was a very strange place for Mommy Amy. She struggled with what she had given up—the career ambition, the drive to accomplish, and the exploration of life's adventures. Younger Amy had always been a dreamer, a planner. It was unusual for her to go a day without a goal.

And Mommy Amy hoped deep down that someday she would return to a professional career, whatever that might be. But she also worried if she would have one to go back to.

Mommy Amy found that everything she did was for someone besides herself. Long gone was the idea of motherhood that she had daydreamed about that day at the company conference table. In reality, motherhood was HARD. And she felt her brain going to mush. She knew she needed to find a better balance for herself and her family, but that elusive goal was challenged by every temper tantrum, missed nap, and illness that entered her home. She had no control over anything, it seemed.

But as her children grew, so did the opportunities for Mommy Amy. Sure, she made tons of mommy friends and could throw an all-star play date: homemade playdough, banana bread, and Baby Mozart playing in the background. But once her oldest started preschool, it was game on. Suddenly, it was time to put those professional skills to work. Cape flapping behind her, with a glint of determination and a smile, Super Mommy was born.

In the years that followed, it was as if she had decided to single-handedly defy her generation's anthem of choosing to juggle the demands of paid work and active motherhood. She knew quite quickly that she didn't want to do both. She aimed to prove she could be happy in "just" motherhood, in her own way, without the big career. Since hanging up the corporate Cape, she had found many ways for herself and her family to thrive.

She managed the finances and marketing for her husband's cabinet business. Taught professional development classes once a month at the university in town. Volunteered at her children's schools. Served on the PTA and Site Council.

Matt, Amy, Emily & Colby Irvine, Monterey, CA, July 2004.

Organized PTO cake walks, and wine parties to benefit local charities. That is, on top of managing her home (she hated cleaning), her family finances, and all the fun things that come with raising kids. Coached youth soccer, hosted moms' nights out and Cabi parties (she modeled clothes, too), and put on annual parties at her house and their cabinet shop.

She taught herself to be a gourmet cook and practiced nightly for her family. Spent time with her mom and grandma, who had moved to her town. Planned adventures and vacations for her family. Enjoyed a weekly date night with her husband. Planted and tended a vegetable garden. Squeezed in working out and running, played adult softball and soccer, and ran half-marathons. All the while trying to raise emotionally happy and healthy children. Oh…and kept herself healthy and fit. No big deal.

Just as she had thrived in high school and college with a busy and diverse life, so was her life thriving as Super Mommy. She was determined to be so much more than "just" a mom. She wanted to be the hero of her own story, her best self. But as you can imagine, at the end of every day (and often at the start), she felt absolutely exhausted.

And so was the Cape. It was heavy, torn, tattered, and barely able to keep up with Super Mommy. It was neglected, and it seemed to grow heavier every single day. Silently and invisibly, the heavy rocks of perfectionism latched on to weigh down Little Amy's Cape. The older she grew, the harder it felt to fly. But she continued to try. She failed to give up or take off the Cape. *Who am I without the Cape? Who will take care of everything if I don't?*

Super Mommy was physically sick…a lot. Sure, she had grade-school-age kids who brought home every virus there was. But it took many years to connect the dots and finally see the impact that constant stress was having on her physical and mental health. She had been living through a roller-coaster cycle of depression, likely since her postpartum depression after her son was born. But as long as she put on her smile, no one knew. *They can't know. What would they think?* She had to just keep plugging away. Pushing through. How could she possibly quit now? She had proven she was capable of so many things, and people were counting on her. But she was running on empty. Something needed to change.

And that change came in the form of a phone call from an old college friend. She had a job that she thought Amy would be perfect for. It was a role on her team. She would earn a fantastic corporate salary and benefits while working from home. How could she turn it down? Her children were both in grade school. Her family had been paying out of pocket for medical insurance for years. And she and her husband needed to stop running a business together. It wasn't healthy.

So with a sigh of relief, she took the corporate job. It gave her a reason to be able to say no to many of the balls she had been juggling. Well, sort of—it turns out that perfectionism and people-pleasing cannot be changed overnight, or even over years. Especially with the temptations of trailblazing and proving to others that you are more than a label…more than enough as you are.

The challenge in trying to recover from perfectionism while wearing a superhero Cape AND in trying to be the best wife and mom for your children? Well, it's just too sizable a task for any human. Especially when that person thinks they have to do it all alone. The road to being exceptional at everything is filled with potholes and warning signs. But when you are so used to making a broken road work—even after many, many years of traveling on that exact same road—you often miss the warning signs that a cliff is just around the bend.

Super Mommy could easily be its own unique book. You've heard a little about her first decade as Super Mom. But before the end of those first ten years, several plot twists tore through Amy's world, each testing her courage and resilience.

Twist 1: Corporate Layoff

Plot Twist

With the new job, Super Mommy and her family settled into a functioning, stable rhythm. Super Mommy now earned a big salary with medical benefits—the pressure was off the family business as the only income. On top of learning and growing in her career, she enjoyed the flexibility of being able to do all of the things she loved as a mom. Her kids were now old enough to see her succeeding in all areas of life…that is, until the day that stability twisted out the window.

The day President Barack Obama was inaugurated should've been a day filled with extreme optimism and happiness. The president's election reflected a new hope for her life as a modern woman juggling a career and motherhood in the early twenty-first century. However, a phone call that morning sent her hopes into a downward spiral. Her company was experiencing layoffs (a reduction in workforce), and her position had been eliminated.

Watching the first Black man become the president of the United States, she experienced the complete extremes of emotions: fear for her own next steps and at the same time, the greatest audacity of hope. How would she balance the duality?

Thankfully, this was not her first plot twist, and she knew how to flex her Cape. She felt confident that she would find a way forward, as she usually did through plot twists. But she was disappointed, sad, and couldn't help but feel rejected. *Why am I not enough? Why couldn't I survive the cuts? What more could I have done in my role to avoid the layoff?*

And to make things even more painful, she had oral surgery scheduled for the next week: gum grafts…in her midthirties. She didn't have a cavity in her mouth, but jaw surgery had led to severe gum recession. She had been warned of the pain she would experience. But she already had pain; she might as well get all the pain over at once.

While recovering from surgery, she found herself feeling all sorts of things. Being idle gave her the time to immerse herself in the grief process. For the first time since her daughter was born, she had felt as if she had it all—she had felt secure. And now, with the loss of the job, she felt frustrated and angry. And she didn't like feeling those emotions.

What was she going to do now? It was the great recession of 2009, and no one was hiring. In fact, every company she knew of was laying off amazing employ-

Pivotal moment

ees, eliminating roles. She had enjoyed the flexibility of remote work and certainly the paycheck and benefits. But if she was honest with herself, she didn't really like the corporate world.

Every time she volunteered in her kids' classrooms, she felt it—the magic. Her Cape felt as if it lit up with a glowing magic. It radiated warmth and made her smile. It was a magical joy that she had yet to feel in a job, other than when she taught college communications or facilitated professional learning at the university.

In college, she had interned in a fifth-grade classroom and had loved the experience. It confirmed the joy she had assumed she would feel as a teacher. However, College Aim was told she could be "so much more than just a teacher." No one wanted to support a teaching career path for her then—and at the time, she was young enough to listen to the advice of others. Even when the magic in other career choices was hard-pressed to be found.

But she was older now. What was stopping her now? Why couldn't she make an old dream come true? What if she went back to school to earn teaching credentials? If not now, while her kids were younger, when would she do it? And at just the thought of her being the teacher in her own classroom, the Cape started to glow. She felt the magic begin to ignite.

While she still felt terrible pain in her mouth, her sadness disappeared. A clarity emerged in her mind. She could vividly picture herself leading a classroom full of students, which activated her optimism. She felt the universe align with her dream—every step she took towards it, she encountered a green light. And within a month, she was enrolled in a teaching-credentials program. She was making it happen.

Within thirteen months, she had completed her California teaching credential. She applied for a job at her children's school, and her dream became a magical reality. Mrs. Irvine taught fifth grade at her children's school. She truly felt like a super teacher. And she embraced the impact she could make on the lives of her thirty-one students. She was born for this… and her Cape was happy, too.

Amy & Emily Irvine, first day of school, Patwin Elementary School, Davis, California, September 2011.

Every single day she showed up in her classroom, she appreciated that she was living her calling. She had never been happier. She could easily teach for the rest of her life. But, sadly, it wasn't meant to be. During her first year of teaching, she received a pink slip, but it was eventually rescinded. However, the pink slip she received her second year would lead to the end of her dream job. That same year, her life became a country song.

Twist 2: Divorce

Unfortunately, her marriage did not survive her dream job. The family business fell apart without her, and

Plot Twist

some very bad choices were made. She lost trust. And no effort was being made to help repair it. She felt devastated and helpless.

A child of divorce, it was the very last thing that Little Amy had ever wanted for herself as an adult or for her children. But irreconcilable differences could not be repaired. Telling both of her children the news of the divorce left her absolutely heartbroken. And as she watched her husband move out of their home, the country song was just getting started.

A month later, they had to euthanize their beloved sixteen-year-old Lab/border-collie mix, Lucy—their "first child." A few months after that, she was given a pink slip from her dream job. Her classroom had been her refuge during the hardest year of her life. Then, her wallet was stolen out of her classroom, and her washing machine stopped working.

And a few months after that, she learned the house would have to be sold—the only house her kids had ever known. She and the children needed to find a new place to live, on top of processing the loss of her marriage, her dog, and her dream job. It's no wonder Momma Amy felt terribly depressed, alone, and scared.

She knew her children needed her to figure out the best next-step options for her little family of three. Living in a college town made finding affordable rental homes in her neighborhood impossible. The houses she could afford to rent were geared more for college kids. *Where in the world is my family of three supposed to go*? It was totally up to her to figure it out—she needed to be the hero for her kids and her.

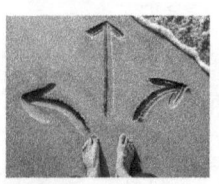
Pivotal moment

Her Cape seemed to understand that she needed help. It activated her imagination to help process this rather huge crossroads of life, a true pivotal moment. She tried to imagine a life in the same town, now, as a different family than everyone knew them to be. Her view of that path brought nothing but stress and sadness. Their family was well-known throughout the town. *Who are we going to be now? How will we thrive in the shadow of our former "successful" selves?*

Perhaps it really was time to consider a fresh start—a different path in a new town with new people, new schools, new sports teams, new grocery stores, and new selves. A fresh chapter to figure out their new identity as a family and as individuals. The idea felt both terrifying and liberating. She felt the universe's pull towards the unknown.

In this new normal, what will success or happiness look like for the three of us, or for their dad and his soon-to-be other family? Mommy Amy was tortured, and everything felt out of her control. The Cape seemed to have disappeared along with the fifteen pounds she had lost during that first year of separation. And they weren't healthy pounds—she had no physical strength or energy. And she couldn't remove the black cloud over her mind that refused to provide a glimpse of light.

Throughout that extremely difficult year, the only time she felt her Cape on her back was when she greeted her students every morning. And, thankfully, her daughter was one of them. After a quick therapy session with her next-door teacher and bestie, she'd wipe her tears away and open the door to her fifth-grade classroom as Super Teacher's brave, smiling face appeared.

Teacher Amy's students gave her purpose and predictability. And her classroom became her safe haven. Yet once the last student left the classroom at the end of each day, the Cape's strength seemed to disappear. After the door closed in the afternoon, the Cape seemed to slide off her shoulders. She reluctantly headed back to a house filled with excruciating happy memories and a future unknown.

In those very dark days, she found she could only process life about five minutes at a time. She was in sheer-survival mode.

By the end of 2012, the sale of their family home was complete. Another family would build their own life in her house. And at the same time, the divorce was finalized. *Now what?* She felt a grief unlike anything she had ever imagined thus far. Super Mommy's own "perfect" little family, as they had known it, ended.

She still had a shot at being called back to teach. But with the divorce, she wouldn't make enough money to raise her kids on her income alone. She knew it was time to return to the corporate world—it was the only way to create financial stability. She found a way back in to an old company as a consultant—thanks to the professional network she had built and nurtured. She had to do what she had to do. And she was absolutely determined to make it work all by herself.

Her children had lived a very lovely—some would call it easy—childhood in that sheltered little town. They knew everyone, and everyone knew them. Their world had been safe, secure, and predictable. Until it wasn't.

Sadly, it felt eerily similar to Little Amy's life. In fact, her son was the same age that she was when the divorces happened. She absolutely hated the pain, fear, and uncertainty that came into their lives with the divorce. But it was what it was. And all three of them needed her Cape, her optimism, and her ability to open windows and turn them into doors.

She did her best to prepare her children for the changes ahead, calling the move a sabbatical, a six-month trial in a new place. It was the best option she could find. And she was resolved that they would all walk through this window turned door with confidence and optimism. She knew the children would learn and grow with her. And all she could do was try her best to love them and to serve as a role model through it all.

So in January of 2013, two weeks after Christmas, Amy and her children moved to another town about a half hour from their university town. It was one of the scariest things she would ever do—leaving a place where everyone knew their name. As they drove away from their childhood home, she felt an uncanny déjà vu. It looked as if she and her children were being transported straight back into the past, to a similar move several decades prior. They looked as sad as she felt to say goodbye to this home, this neighborhood, this school, and this life. They sat quietly pensive as they drove away.

Yet, wouldn't you know, the minute they got on the freeway, the chatter began about what was to come; the possibilities took over. Her optimistic preparation had worked, just as her mom's had for Randy and her all those years ago. Her children began to talk excitedly about the new house, the new school, the new friends, the new normal that they would build together. They put on such brave, optimistic faces.

And when she looked back in the rearview mirror, she gasped. Concerned, her kids asked what was wrong, but she simply smiled. *Nothing's wrong. I'm just so proud of you. And excited for our future.* But as she looked in the rearview mirror, she could see each of her children's sweet little Capes tied tightly around their necks. She smiled again. *Can they feel them draped across their shoulders? Have they discovered them yet?*

Her children had certainly already lived with confidence and courage in their young lives—so many tries with successes and failures. But this big twist to their world was going to require incredible resilience, optimism, faith, and bravery. And she felt a great calm wash over her when she witnessed their Capes had activated.

I can almost picture the three of us, our Capes flowing behind us, driving the minivan into our new town, new home, new school, new sports teams and activities, new friends, new lives. The change requires great bravery, courage, and faith in ourselves. And it definitely requires hope. Can this new life bring great healing? Space to grow and become our authentic selves without the weight of old expectations?

She had to believe that she would figure it all out, one day at a time. That she and the kids would be okay. She held tight to the new life she had imagined. Surviving change was becoming part of her DNA.

Part 3 ~ Serious Adulting

Chapter 12

Single Mom

Becoming a single parent was definitely the start of some serious adulting. Single-mom life was not foreign territory to Amy. She certainly knew how hard it would be in the years ahead. She had watched her own mom navigate adulting while raising her brother and her.

With no college degree and on a secretary's salary, her mom had worked her rear off to raise two kids by herself. And while Amy felt anxiety about being able to succeed while parenting on her own, Amy's tenacity, education, and professional experience certainly gave her advantages, especially financial ones, that her mom never had.

And while Single Mom Amy didn't have a dad to turn to for support, she did have generations of female strength behind her. Her grandma and mom were certainly never going to let Amy and the kids truly struggle. They were not wealthy, but they could serve as financial backup when emergencies came along. But as you can imagine, the last thing Amy wanted to do was ask them or anyone else for help. She wanted to prove that not only could she do this, but ever the competitor, she could set the standard for how to do it.

Anyone how has experienced the loss of a family member, either by divorce or death, knows that surviving the change requires a little dose of Dory from the "Just Keep Swimming" scene of the Disney movie *Finding Nemo*. And if you are familiar with Maslow's Hierarchy of Needs, you know that the foundational layer of human survival means managing basic needs like shelter, food, water, and sleep. And in the early years of her divorce, Amy could muster only enough energy for basic survival—her children's and her own.

For the first time in her motherhood, Single Mom Amy's parenting goals were quite simple. She had to mentally and emotionally turn off the swirl of other people's perceptions of her family's "disaster scene"—the death of her family as they'd all known it. Instead, she had to focus on what she could control at any given moment. And it sure wasn't much.

For a recovering overachiever and perfectionist, imagine how difficult it must have been to let go of the controls in the midst of survival mode. How could she avoid succumbing to the pressure, the temptation to overachieve, to be exceptional at this change? The Cape was challenged by all the plates Amy was trying to spin by herself. But, half the time, she had no idea what she was spinning.

Super Mommy had always been intentional about helping her children build healthy minds. And that meant the duality of cheering for their capabilities while coaching them through their chal-

Amy, Emily & Colby Irvine, Lake Tahoe, 2012.

lenges and failures. She wanted them to experience the wins and losses—with her nearby, of course, to remind them to keep flying. She wanted them to believe in themselves and to become equipped with experiences that helped them stretch and grow while building confidence and courage.

Yet she realized that it was her growing children who must vocalize what they needed and wanted—even if they changed their minds down the road. Just like their mom, they seemed desperate to own some control over their reality and choices. And while she couldn't take away the pain of the divorce, nor put their old family back together, she could help them grow through the change. She very much hoped that this first big plot twist for her children would prove to reveal the strength of their own Capes.

This family of three left a community of people, some of whom questioned and doubted her decision to move. While she tried to focus on the encouragement of her supporters, it was the critics who fueled her determination. Just because her marriage ended, that didn't mean she had lost her intelligence or common sense. She felt confident that, given the options, she had made the best choice for her family. As with anyone who has experienced divorce and the changes it brings, her true friends revealed themselves quite quickly. The others…well, as disappointed as she felt, she couldn't control what they thought.

She had learned that what other people thought of you was none of your business. But the perceived judgment hurt. Of course, it did. These people had no idea what she was dealing with. Just because she physically looked good on the outside—having lost fifteen pounds from the stress—she was very far away from okay. Her true friends knew she was barely breathing. Yet, just as when Little Amy was told no, the judgment she felt during her separation only ignited her desire to succeed. She and the kids would not only survive this change, but she would make sure that they thrived…eventually.

As she and her children began their new life in the new house in the new town, the Newly Single Mom felt the universe give her an unexpected thumbs-up and a high five. Serendipitously, they found the perfect rental home and secured it at just the right time—the neighborhood school opened up two spots in the exact grades her children needed.

From the wonderful friends her children immediately made, to their superhero teachers who sheltered them under their wings and the families who happily welcomed all three of them into their community, it felt as if the universe was saying, "Yes, girl, this is the way. You've got this."

From soccer and baseball, to volleyball and dance, Single Mom was determined to get her kids back into enjoying the activities of their old lives in an attempt to find some semblance of normalcy in the midst of the change. But when she tried to enroll her daughter, the lifelong dancer, in the local dance company, Emily said no.

Her sweet girl told Single Mom that she was done dancing—and no amount of discussion changed her mind. Amy knew that change was hard, and her daughter was at a rough preteen age. And since her daughter wouldn't open up about her feelings, Amy could only guess the reasons for her decision. She had hoped that dancing would help her find her joy and assist in the assimilation into her new community.

The loss of her daughter's sparkle activity broke Single Mom. She would terribly miss watching her daughter perform. Dancing had been her gift for so long; she absolutely shone onstage. And it gave her such a positive outlet for self-expression. Yet she realized that it was her growing children who needed to vocalize what they needed and wanted—even if they changed their minds down the road. They were desperate to find control over their choices, just as their mom felt. So she had to respect her daughter's choice.

This new life in the new town was a chance for both of her kids to release the old expectations of who they were and chart new paths for themselves. While her daughter wanted to leave dance in the past, Amy encouraged her to try new activities like volleyball and softball. She didn't expect her daughter to be a star of either sport—she just hoped her girl would find her people and feel a sense of community once again.

Amy was determined that her children realize they were not alone in experiencing hardships. As humans, we all struggle with life-changing plot-twist events like the aftermath of divorce, the death of a parent, the loss of a home or job. These painful life changes bring about the need for a new normal, a new sense of self, a new identity. A new normal requires a new definition of success, and Amy was still trying to define her own. While, for the kids, she tried to stay positive throughout the changes, on the inside, usually while staring at the ceiling and trying to fall asleep, all her doubts and fears flooded in.

Being a single mom in a town of intact families is a hard thing to do. But between school and sports, she and the kids made new friendships quickly and, indeed, found a new community. While they maintained great friendships from their old town, each of them built new circles of friends, especially from their sports teams. Coaches and parents—men and women—who genuinely cared for her kids and Amy.

They say it takes a village to raise kids. No one feels the value of that village more than a single parent. And as much as she hated to ask for help, the longer she navigated things alone, the more she needed help. No matter the hit to her defiant superhero status.

Like Gemini, her astrological sign, Amy often felt as if there were two twins driving her Cape. The primary twin dominated her everyday life and was the outwardly optimistic Super Mommy and cheerleader for her children. Sacrificing whatever was needed to focus on their needs. Constantly reminding them how much they were loved and how they could do anything they set their minds to—the hallmarks of her mothering personality.

The other twin, however, was her terribly mean inner critic—let's call her Aimee. She showed up at the forefront of her mind when she felt her weakest and most vulnerable. She activated the sticky gray of depression on Amy's Cape. She thirsted for doubt, fed on rejection, and lived for control. And she was way too good at her job. Aimee was that doubtful, disparaging, self-defeating critic. Yes, she was a total bitch. Someone Amy would never want to be friends with.

Yet Aimee thrived in survival mode. And during her years as Single Mom, she never knew when Aimee might take over control of her Cape. It was exhausting to be on guard and constantly in a battle with her mind. Unwittingly, Amy found herself driven to prove to everyone, and to herself (and Aimee), that she could crush on her own what life dealt her. Could convince Aimee that she could give her kids a healthy and happy childhood…all by herself, dammit. But she was living a crazy irony: while she was determined to create a healthy place for her children, she was setting herself up for an unhealthy and unattainable parenting quest for perfection.

Her absolute top priority remained raising healthy kids, helping them assimilate into their new normal. And many people would likely say she achieved her goal. But the Cape of Exceptionalism rolled at full speed ahead. No matter what life threw her way, she pushed forward through any mental and physical pain. She had no time for it and refused to stop to feel or heal. If she lingered too long in any sadness or pain, she knew Aimee would jump on the chance to take her down.

There was too much at stake for her to stop. No one had told her that when something is too heavy, you should put it down and ask for help. And the inner critic was determined that Amy never learn that. Aimee wouldn't have a job if Amy learned to love herself and accept help.

Amy found herself living in a constant dichotomy: Trying her darndest to raise healthy kids and not place unnecessary expectations on their success, yet celebrating their success in hopes it would show everyone that they were all thriving, that she was succeeding as a single mom. She would prove "them" wrong…whoever "they" were. And she was busy planning a future in which her kids could have almost everything they had in their old lives.

After six months in their new town, Amy and the kids began to imagine buying a home. Both kids wanted to be able to paint their rooms, which was not allowed in the rental home. All three were ready to adopt a new dog. And

Amy wanted to invest in something for her future. She wanted to do this *with* the kids—they would learn how to plan for and make big things happen. They would all share in these achievements.

So they began to look forward to Sundays, the day they headed out to open houses and walk-through models in the new housing developments. Each month, Amy had been putting a little money into a savings account for a down payment. Together, they set four goals: (1) buy a house, (2) get a hot tub similar to the one they had at their old house, (3) adopt a new dog, and (4) buy a new car.

And you know what happens when you give Amy a goal—yeah, she did everything she could to crush it. And her kids did, too. At each step of the process, she explained what was needed next and asked for the children's input. She wanted them to learn, but also to have a stake in the game. When they went shopping, she only had to ask them if whatever they wanted to buy was a want or a need. It reminded them of their goals, and they acted accordingly.

By March of 2015, their sacrifices and good choices paid off. Single Mom and the kids put down a deposit on a brand-new home in a neighborhood down the street from their future high school. And a few months later, they moved out of the rental and into their new house.

Later that fall, they had a hot tub delivered to the backyard. At the start of 2016, they adopted their new puppy dog. And by the end of that year, they purchased a new car. They celebrated by driving to their favorite sushi restaurant. And Amy made a big deal about how their choices together had made their goals a reality.

This was the parenting that she could control—exactly what Super Mommy would have done, too. She spent years wanting to have Super Mommy's energy and drive, while balancing the weight of being a single parent. While she resembled Super Mommy on the outside, on the inside responsibility and obligation dominated her every move and thought. She couldn't release the feeling of being in a fish bowl—constantly observed and judged. How in the world could she possibly ever feel as though she were enough?

Her original parenting style and goals as a mom had not changed. Yet with the reality of divorce, she knew her kids watched her do her thing differently from their dad and stepmom. They were different people with different priorities and parenting styles, different households. And there was nothing she could do but focus on what *she* was doing. Even if it meant learning what to do when the world implodes around you.

She had never needed her Cape of Courage and Capability more than during her life as Single Mom. She did not have the benefit of co-parenting. She would've given anything for a peaceful relationship with the other household, but that was not within her control. So she did her best to give her kids a soft, safe place to land, and at the same time, take care of herself.

Her attempts at Cape care were fairly solid. Some were strategies she had always relied on—for example, running, time with girlfriends, and date nights. She still loved watching sports and playing them, so she found coed soccer and softball teams in the new town. She found community in a women's fitness group, which was similar to the close-knit fun of her sorority back in the day. She found other parents she could parent with, but not many were experiencing life as a single parent. When she found other single moms, she found herself nurturing those relationships even more.

But asking for help was still a physically painful act. She was afraid that people would think less of her—she might lose her hard-won persona. In this new town, she wanted people to see her as a capable, confident Single Mommy still doing everything she would've done had she still been married. But every time someone helped her, it reminded her that she was alone. And she hated being alone.

She was determined that her children see her thrive. When she felt great fear, she whispered her mantra, "The children are watching." As she survived the financial challenges of single parenting, surgeries, layoffs, and heartbreaks, they were watching. She knew they watched her every move, and her reactions to these plot twists and choices during the pivotal moments would shape their own Capes in the years ahead. No pressure, of course.

At the end of the day, Momma Amy did not want her kids to need a Cape of Capability, one so heavily laden with responsibility. And she certainly didn't want them to have a Cape of Courage in the way hers had arrived. She knew they had likely felt their Capes of Courage when they left their childhood town. But she pictured her kids with Capes that gave them the courage to try whatever they dreamed of. Capes that made them feel limitless. Success was whatever they felt in their guts made them their unique little selves.

She imagined nurturing their Capes when she cheered them on as they did the things they loved, or during moments when they demonstrated courage or resilience. She tried to model how to keep going, how to avoid letting the hard things in life keep you down or prevent you from reaching your goals. She taught them to use their resources, to open windows when doors closed. To build and invest in a network of friendships. To work hard but have fun.

She wanted them to learn resilience and build confidence in their own capabilities. But on reflection, she never taught them how to really feel the hard stuff. She didn't model how to really feel and process hard things because no one had ever taught her how to allow herself to feel the pain, feel scared and overwhelmed. How to allow herself to be human. To actually allow the sadness to come and go, just as their joy and happiness did. They just saw her push past those hard feelings and make lemonade.

But life is filled with chances to learn. And sometimes a scary situation can prove life-changing in more ways than one…and for more than the person surviving it. During her daughter's last year of high school, Amy learned how to feel some pretty scary feelings. She learned that she deserved to both wear a Cape and receive help. She found out that though she was a Single Mom, she wasn't actually navigating life single-handedly. And her kids got to watch it all happen.

Chapter 13

The Cape Turned Pink

Can you remember a time when you or your family faced an unexpected crisis or plot twist? Do you recall the people who showed up for you? Who dropped off a casserole, homemade cookies, flowers, or a sweet card? Who offered to pick up the kids from school and keep them through dinnertime, or pick them up from soccer practice so you could cook dinner? Who checked in with you and wanted to know how they could help?

During most of her plot twists, Amy was fortunate to have a small circle of incredible supporters and champions. These people knew how hard she pushed herself, and they tried their best to help her remember her humanity. Most people didn't have a clue about the depression she managed behind the smile of her highly functioning persona. But these people did, and she couldn't have survived without them during this chapter of her life.

But asking for help was like her superhero kryptonite. As a little person, she had been disappointed too many times when asking for help. As an adult, it was easier to do it by herself. She found it easy to come up with excuses for the people who failed to show up. To avoid accepting the reality of their friendships. It was easier to believe that people cared, but were just overwhelmed with their own lives—which was also a real truth. She certainly understood the busyness of parenthood.

Either way, she learned whom she could count on, and she kept those people close. Serious adulting meant that no one else was actually coming to take care of things for her. She was the adult in the room, and she needed to count on her Cape to carry her through. But sometimes, when you least expect it, people can surprise you, and helpers arrive.

One day, in the middle of quietly surviving Single Mom's life, she experienced a plot twist that threatened to become another form of kryptonite. Much to her surprise, it was a challenge that rallied everyone around her. It was just the beginning of a major transformation for her Cape.

No, this twist didn't repair the tears in her Cape's fabric. She would need to learn how to do that on her own. But it did remind her that she was never actually alone, even when she was suffering in her mind.

Plot Twist

One August morning, she woke up to realize her Cape had turned pink! The evening before, she had received the most surreal news that no one is ever really prepared to hear—the results of the biopsy on her left breast. It was cancer.

Upon hearing the news, her mind immediately returned to the times in her life when other bad things had happened. She had always rationalized with optimism. *Well, it could be worse… It could be cancer.* But now it *was* cancer.

Her beautiful cousin Melissa, who was more like a sister, had been diagnosed with breast cancer at the young age of thirty-one years old. Melissa fought cancer on and off for over a decade. She absolutely wore a pink Cape—and showed everyone around her what it meant to live life to the fullest, in spite of horrible pain and fear. But after her cancer spread yet a third time, her most courageous battle came to a tragic end. Her passing had left Amy determined to age with gratitude, for herself and her cousin.

Sitting in shock with her own diagnosis, Amy's thoughts fixated on her cousin. How badly she wished that she could call and talk it through with her. Melissa would know exactly what to say—and it would've likely been something sarcastic and hilarious to make her laugh. She missed her every day, but this day more than ever.

She got up to brush her teeth and wash her face. Looking up at the bathroom mirror, she stopped brushing, in shock. There, reflecting back at her, was her Cape, draped across her back! She hadn't seen it in a really long time—had nearly forgotten about it. Yet, she could only stare at the fabric. The Cape had turned pink. She smiled. Melissa—she was not alone.

Before she spoke with her family about her diagnosis, she needed to understand what she was dealing with. Thankfully, she had activated her network prior to having the biopsy. She reached out to the friends she knew who had battled breast cancer. They were the first phone calls she made.

Thanks to her routine mammograms, they had caught her cancer very early. Yet you can imagine her fears, given all that she watched her cousin endure. It would be many weeks before testing revealed more important details about her cancer—she did not have the breast-cancer gene, as her cousin did. She breathed a sigh of relief for her mom and daughter…and her ninety-four-year-old grandma who had already lost one of her two granddaughters to cancer.

With her pink Cape activated, she went into problem-solver mode, researching her diagnosis, trying to learn and understand all of her options. While obviously afraid, she felt strangely capable. And she radiated a calmness that she'd never felt before in the midst of trauma.

She decided to go public with her diagnosis, with hopes that she might raise awareness and urge others to get their mammograms. And the reaction to her post on social media was an unbelievable outpouring of love and support. No one could believe that she, healthy Amy, had cancer. She hoped that being transparent about her situation could help someone else.

For the first time, after years of struggling silently, she felt immediately supported—all because she was brave enough to share this challenge and let others join her journey. And it felt like a social movement; just about everyone she knew had a connection with someone who had battled breast cancer. And when it hit younger people in the prime of their lives, it seemed even more shocking. People rallied to run 5K races to raise funds to cure breast cancer, after all.

Friends across the different chapters of her life jumped in to offer help and words of encouragement. Suddenly, she felt seen, and she wondered why she had doubted the helpers in her life. It turned out that many people had clearly witnessed the power of her Cape in action over the years. She learned that others found her to be capable and strong. They likely thought she had it all going on by herself. Which she did... But what a gift to learn, while you are still alive, the admiration and love others feel for you.

People shared comments such as, "Cancer messed with the wrong woman!" and "Cancer doesn't stand a chance against you!" She received lovely flowers and cards, countless pink pieces of apparel, even a pink F*#k Cancer baseball cap. Her work colleagues chipped in and coordinated dinner deliveries, flowers, and cards. She felt surrounded by love and support, and was deeply and immensely grateful for her cheerleaders.

But for anyone accustomed to being the helper, receiving and accepting help can be difficult. Very quickly, she began to understand what her fellow pink warriors had described as "the gifts of cancer." For the first time in her life, she had an army of Amy Strong teammates standing side by side with her in her fight, with the pink bracelets to prove it. It was overwhelmingly wonderful.

For someone dealing with a cancer diagnosis, every day can feel like a fortnight with many appointments and decisions to be made. Waiting for test results that guide things in different directions. But she was learning how to accept help and felt elevated by the love and support, which was essential for the days she felt swallowed up by the what-ifs that came with a cancer diagnosis.

Several months later, after making the decision to receive targeted twenty-dose radiation treatment, she began to see a light at the end of the tunnel. She could feel the end of journey just on the horizon. She knew her strength, and she knew she was loved. She had survived, and she felt determined that this experience would change her, would activate the Thrive mode on her Cape. She was determined to take care of herself and not sweat the small stuff.

Until, that is, a very unexpected little plot twist popped up—literally—during her treatment plan. A quarter of the way through the radiation, her doctor pushed down

Plot Twist

too hard, and the radiation port popped out. And it would not go back in.

This radiation oncologist, who knew very well what Amy didn't want, looked at Amy and said, "Well, it's okay. You can just finish with regular radiation."

Shock, fear, and anger crept across the Cape. "Wait… What? No! Absolutely not!" She began to cry.

The nurses in the room looked horrified.

She left radiology and completely fell apart. *This is not my plan!!*

Finally, for the first time since her diagnosis, she sobbed… and sobbed…and couldn't stop sobbing. The hard feelings had been locked behind a secret section of her Cape. The door opened, and the feelings flooded out. She was finally feeling all the hard things, and it didn't stop for several days. The reality of all that she had endured finally set in. And she had no idea what to do next. Helpless was a foreign state for Amy's Cape…but there she was.

Amy thought she had done so well managing the stress. She was determined to stay calm for the people around her. She knew that her family would feel positive as long as she *stayed* positive. Focusing on one day at a time was her plan. But now…

Well, she needed a new plan, and she was suddenly terrified. She didn't know what to do. All she could do was try to activate the Cape in Survival mode. Sadly, it knew how to operate that way all too well.

Like the other plot twists in Amy's life, she was faced with a pivotal moment of choices. She had to be her own advocate. She had to figure this out. *What will give me the best odds of the cancer not returning?*

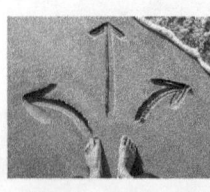
Pivotal moment

Thank God, the pink Cape was still on her back.

Educating herself on additional options, she found a creative solution with the help of her trusted gynecologist, and she listened to her gut. She endured yet another surgery. And four months after her breast-cancer diagnosis, she was pronounced cancer-free!

(*Cue "Survivor" by Destiny's Child.*)

After this last surgery, it seemed that her fight was finally over. She would live…for now. She stopped posting updates for her private Facebook support group. Friends and family took off their pink Amy Strong bracelets, and moved on with their lives. Even the pink on her Cape had begun to fade away.

But Amy's health battle was far from over. Due to the type of cancer, her creative treatment decision was to remove the glands that produce hormones. She also endured a total hysterectomy. As a result of her surgery, at the age of forty-seven, her body went into instant menopause. Compared to the hormonal cliff after childbirth, this was like an 8.0 earthquake along the cliffs of Big Sur. The drop in hormones sent her body into fight-or-flight mode. Her body had no idea how to function without the major organs that had been removed.

She was living in an invisible hell. No one could see the fire and chaos happening inside of her body and on her Cape; it was unlike any crisis or survival mode she had ever experienced. Somehow, she had the sense to keep that pink bracelet on as a reminder to herself. She knew she was Amy Strong. But she had no idea where Amy or her strength had gone.

She woke up every day feeling as if she were hungover or had pulled an all-nighter, which, in a sense, she had.

The insomnia kept her from sleeping more than a couple of hours a night. And after a few weeks, she started to lose some hair. Her nails were breaking, her skin was dry, and she had absolutely no energy.

For someone who had been so in tune with her athletic body her whole life, she didn't recognize her body. She had never felt so unhealthy. She couldn't exercise to work through the stress; she could barely walk up her stairs. She wondered if she would ever feel like herself again.

Months later, when she was healed enough to try working out, she learned the direct correlation between estrogen and the heart. She could no longer control her heart rate—it skyrocketed with an easy walk. And her blood pressure couldn't tolerate bending over. The lumpectomy and radiation had nothing on this.

She didn't want to bother her friends anymore—people had their own challenges and daily lives to balance and get through. And besides, none of her friends had really even started perimenopause. While they were certainly sympathetic and supportive, there was no way to describe the chaos that was her body. No one could relate. And, frankly, she wouldn't be ready to hear about it if they could. And even though the pink had completely faded away, she couldn't even find her Cape.

All she could think about was the suffering that her cousin had endured. She felt horribly guilty for not spending more time helping her, for not checking in more frequently, or for not just showing up at her house with a hug. But when Melissa was first diagnosed, Amy was living a chaotic married life with little babies. She tried to believe that her cousin had understood. But she still felt such sadness now, as she understood some of the pain her cousin had endured.

She chose to channel her cousin's strength to push forward with a persistent hope that she would eventually feel better. She reminded herself, *The kids are watching. They need their strong mom to help them navigate teen life.* And the end of high school for her oldest. And she needed to get back to work! People were counting on her to bounce back. And she desperately needed some sense of normalcy.

While grateful that the cancer was gone, she began to wonder if she'd ever feel happy again. She had asked enough of her pink support squad. So she suffered in misery…quietly…alone. And as it happens, when one pushes hard while simultaneously trying to heal, it took a long time for any sort of normalcy to return. Long gone was the determination she had found while wearing her pink Cape—that optimistic determination to live her life to its fullest in Thrive mode.

Thrive? Her Cape had been stuck in Survival mode for so long it was quickly retriggered with this last surgery. The stickiness of expectations and the smothering of her inner critic took over the Cape. An Off switch could not be found—she was stuck in Survival mode no matter how hard she tried.

With the passing of two seasons, summer arrived. The warmth and sunshine came on slowly, but surely…as did the return of Amy's energy. Her body began to stabilize. The Cape felt lighter. Amy's mojo was coming back; eventually, so did her smile. She started sleeping better, began to exercise regularly again, and started to lose some of the weight she had gained. *Is the worst of the storm really over? Can I finally be heading to the stability of a new normal?*

She saw her oldest child off to college, moved into a new role at work, and focused on helping her youngest navigate the last years of high school and prepare for college. She developed a new routine designed to slowly help her start thriving and enjoying life once again. She felt hopeful.

And she did thrive...for several months... Until a sneaky little virus called COVID-19 spread across the world. Just as she was beginning to plan new flight patterns for the Cape, she was grounded in her house—in lockdown—with the rest of the world. Survival mode reactivated.

And one year into the global COVID-19 pandemic, the Cape reached its limit. Single Mom's greatest fear of all nearly became a reality. Finally, after so many, many years of surviving, the Cape experienced a quiet crash landing. Fog was involved.

Chapter 14

The Slow, Quiet Crash

An early morning in December of 2021

In the haze of a dream, she heard the theme song to the Harry Potter movies—the alarm on her cell phone. As her brain came into consciousness, she pressed Stop on her phone to end the chiming, stretched, and got out of bed. As she ambled to the bathroom to brush her teeth, she heard her partner's voice.

"Amy, I have missed calls from your son's girlfriend!"

She turned to look at his face as she digested his words. "What do you mean? Why would she have called you in the middle of the night?"

As the words began to register, her body froze, and her blood turned ice-cold with panic. She rushed to the nightstand and picked up her iPhone, which, of course, had been set to Mute Notifications overnight. Quickly scanning a long, jumbled string of missed texts and call notifications, she felt her stomach drop. Without clicking to read them, she immediately tried to phone her son. The call went straight to voicemail.

Scanning the phone frantically, but more focused now, she read notifications of missed calls at midnight, frantic texts from his girlfriend, and then a missed call from a Southern California medical center at 2:00 a.m. A rational person might've called his girlfriend next. But there was nothing rational about her frantic state. And she was still half asleep.

She clicked on the missed-call number to return the 2:00 a.m. call. It was a hospital, so of course she was met with a stream of automated message choices: "If this is an emergency, please dial 9-1-1…" Of course, it's an emergency! "Thank you for calling…medical center. If you know your party's extension, dial it now. Press one for directions; press two for the directory…"

What button do you press to find out if your child is still alive?? She nearly gave up, but then she remembered that pressing zero in an automated system usually transferred the call to a live person.

An operator finally answered, "How can I direct your call?"

Trying to remain calm, she said, "I'm trying to find my son. I missed a call last night from this number. My son goes to school there, and I need to find out what happened and where he is."

"What is his name?"

She whispered his name through tears.

Pause…

"I'm sorry, Miss, but we are not allowed to give out information about this patient."

"What??!!!" she screamed hysterically.

"I'm sorry, but he's an adult. He's over eighteen years of age…HIPAA laws, you know."

"But he's my baby boy! He just turned eighteen less than two months ago!"

Pause…

"I'm so sorry…but I can't share any specific details."

She paused briefly, then said, "I *can* tell you he was discharged this morning."

"Oh my God, thank you." She ended the call, curled up in a ball, and cried.

The situation was insane. In just two short months, her child was now considered to be an adult. And as his mother, well, she apparently had no right to know anything about him or his health. At that moment, she remembered the advice from a friend with older kids…something about power-of-attorney forms… *Oh my God, it's my fault for not being prepared!*

After several minutes of sobbing and shaking, a surge of energy came into her body, and a stronger and very determined person took over. It was Mama Bear. The Cape had activated itself.

She jumped up and ran back to pick up the phone to call her son's girlfriend. But before she could make the call, she saw it. Lost in the string of texts was a missed message from her sweet boy. He had sent it just two hours earlier… this morning…not last night… With a strange, terrified hope, she clicked to read the words…

He was so sorry to worry her. He had had a rather eventful night and was going to try to sleep. But he wanted her to know that he was okay.

He is okay.

Staring at his words, his terrified mom realized she had been holding her breath, so she let out a huge sigh. She texted him back, thanking him for the update but asked him to call when he woke up.

But even after she spoke with him, she wasn't convinced that he was okay. She felt a traumatic crisis had been averted for the moment...and she would have to wait another five days, until he finished his finals, before she could see his face.

This plot twist was unlike anything Amy had ever experienced or could have imagined. She had spent two decades as a supermom capable of fixing and solving any family problem. It would take her some time to realize that this problem was not hers to solve...no matter how desperately she wanted to help. Sure, he needed her love, but not even her Cape could help this situation. *Her* magic couldn't fix this situation.

And while there is indeed a dramatic backstory that led up to the hospital visit, and certainly a complex story that followed his return home to the nest, you will have to use your imagination as to how it all went down. While this traumatic plot twist is critical in the timeline of Amy's journey, this is not her story to tell. But she *can* share what happened next in her own life.

In the countdown to Christmas, there wasn't a single morning that she woke up and wasn't gripped by fear and frustration over her inability to help her son. The fear became a palpable fog that refused to budge from the air above her home. There was nothing she could do but pray, which is something she hadn't done in a very long time.

With time, her son's journey to healing began. She felt both immense pride and utter relief. Her baby bird had activated his own Cape and ignited his unique magic. This scary crisis led to the discovery of his own spectacular superpowers. She could only sit in awe and cheer him on.

Yet as his light began to return, his mom's magic seemed to be fading away. One had to wonder if she had been channeling all of her magic into helping to ignite her son's Cape. Once his Cape fired up, did her own initiate shutdown?

The fear-filled weeks had certainly taken its toll on an already tattered and heavy Cape. But even when her fears began to subside, she found that she was far from okay. It felt as if her Cape had landed in a slow, quiet crash. And she couldn't find a bit of magic to bring it back to life.

Momma Aim awoke one morning and was forced to address the fragile state of her mind. For weeks, each day had felt like Groundhog Day…and a relentlessly foggy day, at that. Navigating daily life in a full-blown fog storm felt impossible. Mentally and physically depleted, her immune system shot, the sweet boy's mom came down with the COVID-19…for the first time. And it hit her hard.

Since the beginning of the pandemic in March 2020, she had lived with a quiet terror inside her mind. While she had received vaccinations for the virus, her biggest fear had been what would happen to her if she did contract the virus. With her history of cancer and fragile lungs—asthma and countless bouts of pneumonia—she was horribly afraid of the potential complications from COVID. Frankly, she was terrified of being on a ventilator and not being able to breathe. And she had suffered nightmares about it.

When she thought of what might happen to her lungs, all she could imagine was her sweet, dear cousin. Melissa had fought several recurrences of breast cancer. She required oxygen to breathe, and eventually the cancer took over her lungs. Memories of watching her gasp in her last moments and hearing about the horror stories of people hospitalized with COVID-19...well, it was just too much for Single Mom's overworked survivor mind.

After two positive tests confirmed COVID, she tried her best to isolate herself from the other four people sheltering in her house. While she felt lucky to contract the virus after her vaccinations, she was still hit hard. She got very sick, and her brain couldn't rise above the very thick fog smothering her. While she was able to manage her symptoms at home, all of her helpers were trying to avoid getting sick. So, once again, she had to help herself while continuing to work every day from her home office. She was barely able to get out of bed each morning...the weight of it all just felt so, so heavy.

After three very long weeks, she finally physically began to breathe better. Yet the fog in her brain refused to budge. She couldn't concentrate on anything. She couldn't summon an ounce of energy...couldn't even find a way to smile. Every morning, she woke up with the ongoing fear for her son's safety, coupled with a fear that she herself might be lost forever. It felt like Groundhog Day every single day, and her depression only deepened. She knew depression...had fought the persistently sticky gray on her Cape for many years. But this felt like something entirely different and more catastrophic.

Her first terrible bout of depression occurred postpartum while mourning the loss of her son's twin. But, this time, well, it crept up on her while she was distracted by the needs of everyone around her. The fog was so thick that even her Amy light couldn't stay lit. She knew something was very, very wrong. And she didn't know how she could wake up another day feeling the way she did.

Then, one late afternoon, after yet another ten-hour day spent alone in her office on back-to-back virtual Zoom meetings for work, she simply ran out of fuel. Super Amy was nowhere to be found. She just couldn't function another hour trying to be her old self. She crawled out of her desk chair and sat down on the floor. Her body had caught up to her brain—both tired of living in survival mode.

Underneath her desk, behind her trash can, the bright yellow of a sticky note caught her eye. It looked as if it had stuck to the wall while on its way to finding the trash can. Curious, she reached to grab the note and immediately recognized her own handwriting. Next to a phone number, she had written the words "Mind Coach." With her foggy brain, she tried to recall when that note might have been written…likely several years before. She stared at the note for what must've been quite a while.

For far too long, she had been afraid of her own kryptonite. She couldn't bear to reveal her humanity by asking for help…and tapping out. For some reason, it had seemed okay to accept help during her cancer treatment. But wasn't the state of her mental health a disease as well? Why was she trying to do this alone? Her Cape literally couldn't fly anymore.

She grabbed the sticky note and her cell phone, lay down on the carpet, and in the next moment, mentally surrendered. She knew she couldn't fix whatever was happening to her all by herself. Utterly defeated and very sad, she made the phone call.

You see, Mommy Amy was a lot like the book *The Giving* Tree. She was selfless and giving, with no boundaries around herself. She was conditioned to thrive on fulfilling the needs of others. And at this stage of her life, her branches and fruit were long gone. She'd given them all away, trying to please everyone else. In fact, she had given for so long that she didn't know any other way. And she really felt like the Giving Tree at the end of the story—a lonely old stump.

She doesn't remember what words came out of her mouth when the triage nurse answered her phone call. The only thing she can remember saying is something about not wanting to die, but not being able to wake up another morning feeling the way she felt.

A healthcare provider was rather quickly transferred onto the phone. The recommendation was that she attend an intensive group-therapy program. Unlike her son's virtual program, the doctor preferred that she attend an in-person program, every day for six hours a day. Out of the house. All by herself. Her only responsibility would be to show up each day, wearing her mask (it was still the pandemic), and participate as she was asked.

Even in her terrified, zombielike mental state, the idea of leaving her house every day felt like a surreal, magical gift. Her family would have to take care of themselves. With a deep breath, she took off her Cape and answered the doctor, "Yes, please."

She picked herself up off the floor and walked upstairs to her bedroom. She opened the closet door, placed the Cape on a hanger, and hung it up next to a summer sundress. She likely wouldn't need either for a long, long time.

Chapter 15

Hugging the Kryptonite

What do I wear to mental health group therapy? It had been nearly two years of quarantining during the COVID-19 global pandemic. She had been living in pajamas and workout clothes. She rarely ever left the house, except to walk the dog, go to the grocery store, or put gas in her car.

Her winter pandemic uniform consisted of yoga pants (or pajama bottoms), a hoodie, and a baseball cap. *Why change my wardrobe now?* She went for inconspicuous—she didn't want to stand out. She chose to wear her cozy UGG boots, too. Considering her purses and bags, she hung up her Coach purse and grabbed an old backpack.

Before turning off the closet light, she spotted the old Cape hanging next to her summer dresses. She had worn it for as long as she could remember, especially when she needed courage. That morning, boy, she desperately needed it.

At the same time, though, she assumed that she couldn't get help if she was wearing her Cape—you know, the kryptonite and all. And it was just too heavy. She would have to get through this plot twist on her own. *Since this path is of my own choosing, is it really a pivotal moment?* Either way, she was resolved to live into it without her Cape.

Once she'd agreed to attend the therapy program, the fog seemed to lift enough to take action. It was as if a different person had taken over her mind. She matter-of-factly focused on getting herself to the program. And that meant, for the first time in her life—other than after her pregnancies—she reluctantly took a leave of absence from work, a "medical leave." She had no choice, and she knew it.

When she visualized actually showing up to this program, the true panicking began. Usually, she was prepared before she walked into a meeting, but she had absolutely no idea what to expect in this situation. *What in the world am I going to talk about in front of a group of strangers?* She was a zombie, a shell of her former self. *What drove me to this place of severe depression? Was it the fear of losing my son? COVID? Far too many years of flying for others or proving to others that I am exceptional? And now…well, I certainly feel far from exceptional. What is really wrong with me?* And then the scariest thought: *What will happen if this doesn't help?* She was too afraid to imagine that possibility.

Day one of the program, the alarm on her cell phone woke her up. Thank God, she had set it—she hadn't slept much. Fear pulsed through every fiber of her body. She methodically got dressed—hoodie and sweats. She chose to pull her hair back in a ponytail, fearing a hat might give her a headache. But in reality, she didn't want to show up in a lid from her collection that signaled successful overachiever affiliations. She didn't want people to know that she usually had her shit together. Because if they did, they'd know she was a huge failure.

Of course, she walked out to get into her car and realized that it was raining—pouring, actually. Classic—the universe was crying for her. *But is it judging me, or is it relieved that I am finally letting someone try to help me?*

Pulling into the parking lot, she saw several young people hanging out under the easement of the building, smoking cigarettes. *Wonderful. Totally my type of crowd.*

Walking up to the door, she saw a bell. Reluctantly pressing the bell, she heard a sound, and the front door unlocked. *What the hell? What am I doing here??*

As she turned around to head straight back to her car, she realized there were several people waiting behind her to walk inside. People who looked very sad and irritated that she'd delayed their entrance; they seemed resigned to being there. People who looked as if they struggled to pay rent, hold down a job, or get over their addictions. People trying to get their shit together— *Well, I guess that last part I can relate to.*

Reluctantly shuffling into the main office, she was told to sign in and handed a clipboard with paperwork to fill out. She found a seat and pulled her readers out of her bag. On the verge of tears, she realized her mask was steaming up her readers as she tried to control her breathing. Sweat began streaming down her face, and her heart felt as if she'd just finished a run. *Am I having an anxiety attack?*

Trying to practice yoga breathing, she lifted her head and slowly gazed around the room. Took in the check-in system, the rules on the wall, the Styrofoam coffee cups, the security glass in front of the receptionist… She thought she might vomit. *What in the hell am I doing here? What kind of help do I really need? What am I going to get out of this place?*

It was 42 degrees Fahrenheit outside, but she broke into a cold sweat. Somewhere in the back of her mind, she assumed she was likely in shock, but at the same time, she knew she needed to stay. She must summon the courage of the Cape not on her body. And slowly, but surely, fragments of courage appeared to arrive from deep within, from the depths of her gut.

I can do hard things. She had done and survived many, many hard things before. But this, well, this was a totally new kind of hard; she'd never been through anything like it. *I just don't belong here, do I?* Until…well…she realized that she actually did…

And day one continued to be a memorable one. Group therapy is exactly what you would imagine. A group of people sitting in chairs in a circle, sharing their feelings with each other and the therapist in charge. Just as the therapist began his opening remarks, Foggy Amy accidentally kicked her travel mug of coffee over—the entire cup of freshly brewed coffee spilled across the carpet beneath her chair. Mortified, she looked up to apologize. No one said a word, nor offered to help her clean it up. They simply watched her sheer discomfort as if it were entertainment.

As she listened to various people share what had brought them to this group, she immediately felt even more ridiculous. The "normal" Amy, well, she could've been facilitating this discussion. In fact, she *had* facilitated discussions for a living! Yet, she knew Professional Amy was nowhere near the building. And the more she listened to these people's problems, the more she felt compelled to leave.

One man's wife had just died in a small plane crash, along with her sister, father, and brother-in-law. Another man with an online-gambling addiction had lost all of his family's money. A young woman her own daughter's age was fresh out of rehab; *her* mother was an addict living on the streets. Another young man, also just out of rehab, had just tried to jump off a bridge.

Thank God, I left the Coach purse at home.

While there may not be a Crisis Olympics, her troubles felt rather silly in comparison to these people's. In fact, at one break, she almost left before it was her turn to speak. She would have, had it not been for the man whose wife had died in the plane crash. He, somehow, could see her pain and encouraged her to stay.

When the time to speak was hers, Capeless and terrified, she began to share the story of her son—his slow, quiet crash, what happened, and what almost happened. She shared how terrified she felt about life. How extremely lost she felt. How her brain no longer felt as if it were her own. How completely exhausted she was from just having to be herself.

When she started to cry, a kind woman handed her a box of tissues. After her turn, she leaned back in her chair and wondered who had just spoken. Sure, she had, but it felt like an out-of-body experience. Fragile, paralyzed, and tearful, she survived that first group session. Later, she realized that she had allowed her younger selves to do the talking for her—they were far more compassionate than the Amy living into such serious adulting.

And after her second group session, a light began to glimmer in her mind, moving away some of the fog. She was beginning to understand why a group experience like this was effective. As it turns out, one of the "gifts" of group therapy is actually comparisons. No, not in the competitive Olympic scores or medals sense. But when you see and hear the sadness and despair of other people and their stories, it cannot help but bring perspective into your own life. At the same time, you develop an empathy for the other people who are so bravely sharing and processing their pain. Trust begins to build, and members of the group respond to each other as much as they do to the therapist.

In turn, this compassionate group experience allowed Fragile Amy the space to start processing events and feelings she had bottled up for far too long. This place and these people, whom she had so arrogantly judged upon first arriving, ended up becoming a safe haven, a community of healing and hope. They sat with her tears and fears. They helped her feel some very scary and painful feelings. They rooted for her to find her way back. And she will forever be grateful to them all.

One Monday morning, many weeks into her experience, a counselor who had been gone for a week came in to lead a session. He turned to her and said, "Hi, welcome to the group. What is your name?"

Staring at him with surprise, she said, "David, it's me, Amy." And then the shock was his.

She hadn't realized the progress she was making. Hadn't noticed the new energy she found in the morning to put on makeup and style her hair. But David saw it! And he saw her smile—the genuine Amy smile that had been covered by the fog. Now, sitting before him, she looked like a totally different person. The way she sat and carried herself. She didn't resemble at all the Amy who barely crawled into the building that first day.

David was amazed and so happy for her. He told her she was ready to leave the group program.

Digesting this information was a slow, strange process. *Leave? But wait... Is he sure? Am I really ready? Maybe it's too soon. What will happen if I leave? What if I fall right back into my old patterns of behavior?*

She had come to rely on the predictable routine, the people, the change of getting out of the house and focusing just on herself. She wasn't sure she was ready to give that up. But she could transition to a virtual group and continue to have the weekly support of a therapist.

Slowly but surely, she found her way back to a clearer mind with the help of medication, cognitive-behavior therapies, in-person connections and community, and the release of pain from her body and mind. She reemerged a lighter, clearer, and certainly more determined Amy. Determined to change some aspects about how she lived her life—especially establishing of boundaries. She knew it was time to show herself the love and priority that she had shown everyone else in her world. She was learning how to love herself.

She was recovering from the trauma with her son, the pandemic, a lifetime of plot twists and traumas...all while managing her long COVID depression. Sure, she was equipped with strategies to clear the gray when it showed up. But, even more, she was recovering from a lifetime spent trying to live as a fictional character in a very real human world.

And here's the funny thing: as group began that final day, she felt totally capable of running that support meeting on her own. She had facilitated group discussions for as long as she could remember—even taught small-group communication in college. She felt the strength of her younger self. And, most importantly, she felt capable once again of being herself. She didn't need to save everyone in that room. She just needed to save herself.

And if she really was a superhero, even Superman had his kryptonite. A green mineral that originated from his home planet, this kryptonite caused the comic-book character to become weak when he was exposed to it. It was the thing that took his superpowers away.

It turns out that during the group experience, she uncovered her true fear—her kryptonite. She wasn't afraid of asking for help itself. She feared not being prepared to manage life when the worst hit. Not being able to save the day or be the hero. She really feared disappointing other people. *But why do I always have to be the one who knows what to do? Why do I always have to be the one counted on?*

Older Amy feared losing her powers if she took off the Cape and asked for help. She had avoided doing that for as long as she recalled. And who would she be without her superpowers? But she learned that her magic was something that could not be extinguished by anyone but herself.

And by choosing to go to group—asking for and receiving help—she had chosen to embrace her kryptonite. To feel the magic in being cared for. Supported and respected, even when she felt her most vulnerable and least like a superhero.

She was still Amy. Vulnerability and fragility just signaled the need to recharge her superpowers. A time to hug the kryptonite. Show compassion for herself. Let others help her process the challenges of life. And she realized, with much peace, that she would never again have to be alone in her mind.

While wearing her Cape, she was enough for everyone who needed her. She focused on pleasing others, taking care of others the way she had hoped her father would do for her. By putting others, like her children, first, they would never have to feel less than enough. She thought that was her superpower. But to heal, she had to accept that she alone was more than enough, whether or not she was wearing her Cape. Acceptance—that was the greatest gift she could give herself. Accepting herself as being enough as she was, well, that gave her back her superpowers.

Given the magic and impact of the group experience, naturally, she very much hesitated to leave this sanctuary. They spoke a language of self-love and healing. They didn't expect her to be a superhero for anyone but herself. After hugging goodbye her peers, doctor, therapists, and staff, she cautiously walked out the door, ready to reenter the world.

She got into her car, and, just before putting on her sunglasses, she caught a glimpse of herself in the rearview mirror. The woman looking back at her appeared really familiar. Yes, there she was, hopeful and determined. But much calmer and wiser. More intentional with her energy. She knew it was finally time to take care of herself. She never wanted to crash-land again.

Embracing this midlife awakening, it was finally time to consider what Little Amy needed. And that meant, well, finding her first.

Part 4 ~ Midlife Awakening

Chapter 16

Finding Little Amy

So the quest began to find Little Amy. Midlife Amy couldn't shake the clarity of the instructions that her doctor had given her years before. *What does Little Amy need right now?* Midlife Amy knew, in her gut, that finding her younger self was critical to her future.

After the slow, quiet crash, she knew there was no way to keep living the way she had been trying to survive during her Single Mom decade. Something, or things, needed to change. She had only just uncovered the magic of self-love, and she was determined to continue reinforcing her new healthier boundaries. She needed to feel fearless about changing her mindset, but she certainly knew that change was hard.

Can I really attempt a transformation without my fearless Cape? If she attempted to wear it again, how could she shift the Cape's primary diet from Survival mode to a balanced approach when paying attention to her inner voices?

Truthfully, she couldn't recall what it felt like when Little Amy wore the Cape. Yet she believed Little Amy could tell her the origin of her magical powers. She could explain what it meant and felt like to imagine, think, and live as her authentic self. She had to find her little self.

She began by learning to put up boundaries around herself. Without a Cape, she stopped believing she could save the day for everyone around her. But it was hard because helping others had been her love language, her identity. The practice of enforcing boundaries would likely be a lifelong journey, but she knew she had to try. And she used to be really good at trying.

Without wearing her hero's Cape, and without needing to have all the answers, she found herself embracing her learner's mindset. When she was younger, she loved to learn. So she tried on her curiosity once again.

She sought out people who reminded her of her usual high energy and positive self. Listened to the wisdom of their podcasts and read their books. She practiced talking to herself as if she were her younger self, or even one of her children. And she made it easier by posting photos of her younger selves around the house. She couldn't avoid them, and she certainly couldn't be mean to them.

She found a new mind coach who helped her return to Little Amy and remember what made her lovable and certainly more than enough. They worked forward from her childhood to understand what had complicated the Cape of Courage and began processing the plot twists and pivotal moments that had built Little Amy's character. In the process, she learned to forgive herself and to accept who she was today without the Cape. While getting reacquainted with Little Amy, she remembered all of the wonderful things about wearing her Cape. The confidence she felt, the courage she had in tough situations, the wisdom her Cape carried from her past experiences.

She slowly began to come out of her pandemic shell and connect with friends whom she had missed. People who loved her, who understood the challenges of living with her Cape—especially the gray layers—and who knew her younger selves. And she began to form a picture of how others might have seen her younger self. She was surprised. Many people who had watched her soar in life told her they thought of her as a superwoman who could do anything. And they didn't even know about her Cape!

She was lucky to spend time with her mom, looking through old photo albums and asking her questions about Little Amy. "Mom, was I always pretty fearless?"

Her mom smiled. "Yes, you really were."

As her mom told stories about her fearlessness, she could see why Little Amy imagined herself wearing a Cape. She had really been daring and determined, and had often turned her imagination and dreams into reality. That's what had made her Little Amy.

Older Amy wanted to rediscover her imagination. She reread some of the books that Little Amy had loved, returning her mindset to those characters who had inspired little Amy to dream. *Have I lost my imagination? The ability to dream? Or is it just buried under the layers of responsibility and adulthood?*

And as she immersed herself in the stories of her youth, her imagination slowly returned. She began dreaming of places to go and people to meet. And sorting through old books, she found gold at the bottom of a box—her old journals. She found the words of younger Amys staring back at her from the pages. Journaling her feelings, dreams, disappointments, and inner deep thoughts had always been Little Amy's way of processing her world. Writing was just something she always did. All of the other Amys had written in journals. Words came easily—drawing did not!

Reading Little Amy's thoughts made her realize that she could still hear her young voices; they returned to her through the pages of her very own journals. The pages told the stories of her plot twists and pivotal life moments, as well as her everyday challenges and dreams. Reading the pages felt as though she were getting reacquainted with an old friend. And the more she read, the more she realized the power that writing had brought to her younger selves. While she had often felt alone in her mind, writing allowed her to be a friend to herself.

Through the words on each page, the voices of her younger selves sounded clearly powerful. While they expressed emotions and frustrations, disappointments and heartaches, they also revealed the resilience and determination that sat front and center in her mind. And here she thought those qualities had only lived on the Cape itself.

The journals turned out to be the treasure she didn't know had been missing. They were proof of the powers that had always existed within her. Hopefully, they had only grown more powerful with age. Reading her own words from the past, she felt totally inspired by her little self. And she felt grateful for the clarity she found. She had never really been alone—even if it felt that way sometimes in her mind.

She remembered the powerful love and lessons from the people in her life. For example, her very brave and courageous mother, who had both demonstrated how to be resilient and capable, and encouraged her daring dreams. Her grandparents and her GG, who represented the steady rocks of stability and love for her family. Her amazing brother, the one consistent, positive male presence in her life, who thought she could do anything, and likely still did.

She remembered the many dear friends who had encouraged and supported her throughout all of the different seasons of her life. All of these people who had very likely tried to tell her that she was more than enough. But she couldn't seem to hear them. There was too much noise telling her otherwise.

She carried too much self-doubt and too many memories of disappointment and sadness, of not feeling worthy enough to be loved for who she was. That old pain had always served as red-flag reminders to always be prepared, to be on guard, to don her armor as protection against anything that could potentially cause her pain. Yes, she had taken herself way too seriously.

The journals painted a landscape of a typical girl's life—one filled with both daring and self-doubt. And while revisiting the stories of her youth, she felt sad for her younger selves. They had put so much pressure on themselves. They hadn't realized, at the time, how often they had chosen bravely and wisely. How many times they had owned very adult decisions and succeeded. They couldn't celebrate their own hero's journey because they were so worried whether other people would approve of them. There was always that one person she wasn't enough for; he kept her pushing, always prepared to prove him wrong.

What if she had been able to tell her younger selves that they truly were HER hero? And with that thought alone, she cried. Her quest had worked. Deep in her soul, she felt the wisdom acquired across her life as Amy. She took a deep breath. Exhaled.

Older Amy felt inspired. She would sit with this wisdom and give herself the coaching she had always needed. She would continue to learn more about her younger selves. And she would find a way to heal Little Amy, wherever she was. In the meantime, she would do things that Little Amy loved—running, dancing, playing, and laughing.

And, one morning, while out on a run, she found her. The determined, happy girl with the ponytail swaying. In the shadow before her, she couldn't see the wrinkles on her face or the gray in her hair. She only saw the shape of Little Amy. The girl who knew she could do anything. She had never left—she'd been inside of her all along.

Older Amy was beyond excited to see her little self. She was real! She felt instantly inspired by her. And she wanted to learn more. What were her dreams, her imagination, her world of endless possibilities?

She now understood the meaning of self-love and self-care. What it felt like to put her needs above those of others. To put her oxygen mask on first and not feel selfish doing it. And just then, she knew what she had to do.

She very much wanted to wear her Cape! But it needed a serious redesign. Over all the years, she had never made the time to repair it or let it heal before she attempted her next flight. She knew that pushing through pain and stress for so long had brought toxic stickiness and weight to the Cape. The gray stickiness of sadness and unrealized expectations had stretched holes in the fabric. The stickiness of other people's expectations had never been removed.

It was time to examine the Cape. Repair the tears and broken stitching. Clean off the stickiness, dirt, and dust. Show her Cape the love it had given her. It deserved her attention and love. If she was going to thrive as her future selves, she needed a Cape that would be cared for and nurtured, just as she needed to love and care for herself.

But self-love also meant feeling enough for who she already was. And she still didn't really know how to feel that way. But, now or never, it was finally time to figure it out. No one was coming to save her. She had to save herself.

Chapter 17

Layers

Little Amy had always wanted to be the hero of her own story. Embarking on her journey to find her younger self had ignited this recollection so vividly that Midlife Amy knew it had to be true. Now that the memory and state of mind was reawakened, she felt resolved to keep the flame alive for as long as she lived.

How could I have forgotten how magical the world seemed to Little Amy? How could I have forgotten what it felt like to live with such curiosity, with such an optimistic imagination?

Older Amy desperately wanted to learn how to be more like Little Amy. And she had to believe that the fearless magic of her youth might be found somewhere within her old Cape. That torn, tattered, and heavy version—with the crazy people-pleaser stitching. Sure, it had helped Amy to persist and survive, even in the face of relentless self-doubt, fear, and loneliness. It also carried the strength and confidence she gained from her plot twists and pivotal moments. And she wanted to retain that wisdom—it was a superpower.

But her Cape deserved to be appreciated for all that it had endured. Refreshed to remove the weight of years of neglect. Examining her Cape would likely force her to face and feel some of the really hard stuff. And she'd learned at group that holding in the hard feelings had made the Cape heavier. So maybe it was time to release some hard things. And she certainly knew how to deal with hard things.

In this midlife awakening, she was seeing the Cape with a clear, fresh perspective. She knew it was time to offer compassion to her Cape, to learn to love it as it was. Yet at the same time, she must find ways to heal it and provide better daily care for it. *And if I don't do this now, when in the world will I heal? If not now, then when?* Her future selves needed her to find the source of her fearless magic.

And so, channeling fearless Little Amy, Midlife Amy took a deep breath, walked into her closet, and pulled her Cape off the hanger. She carried the Cape downstairs and gently spread the fabric out on top of her kitchen table. She felt her jaw clench—there was shame in seeing the neglect. She felt frustrated that she had allowed this to happen.

Why did I continue to push myself so hard for so long? Feeling compassion for her younger selves, she resolved to do better.

Grabbing her readers and some sewing scissors, she got to work. Looking at the back of her Cape, she was surprised to realize how much better it looked than it had felt on her back. The shiny blue-satin fabric sure looked beautiful—light and effortless. Confused, she turned the Cape over to examine the inner lining.

And as often happens, it took looking inward—at the inside lining of the Cape—to realize where the damage had occurred. The Cape's shiny blue fabric reflected what the world saw on her back, from the outside. But seeing the Cape's inner lining, well, she felt as if she were peering behind the Wizard of Oz's curtain.

Midlife Amy found herself staring at what could only be described as a grain-sack material. Adjusting her readers to examine the fabric more closely, she realized that a sticky, gumlike paste was splattered all over the charcoal-gray material. And she could only laugh at the trim that had been holding it all together—duct tape.

Talk about survival mode, she thought. *No wonder the Cape was so uncomfortable to wear for so long.*

Staring at the tattered inner lining of her Cape, she made a connection—it bore an uncanny similarity to her recent state of mind. No wonder she had felt so uncomfortable in her own skin. *Of course…I felt so gray, sad, and uninspired by life. No wonder I didn't have any magic left to share with the world or myself.*

Throughout her life, it had taken a lot of energy to ensure she was appropriately dressed beneath the Cape for whatever obligation she was fulfilling or attempting. She had been so busy taking care of other people's needs and caring for their Capes. But she had never thought to look at the inside lining of her own. *No wonder my own Cape went from something magical to something that belonged in the garbage.*

And she felt like such a fraud. She had been walking around, the picture of confidence and capability, while wearing this shiny magical Cape. People could only see her capable achievements and the Cape's shiny outer fabric. But on the inside, literally, she was just barely held together.

Staring at this survival inner layer, she knew something else must lie beneath it. *There must be more.* Channeling her relentless perseverance, she vowed to dig through whatever it took to uncover the original fearless lining of Little Amy's Cape. After all, this was the same Cape of her childhood. And in fifty years of life, she had certainly faced plenty of challenges and plot twists that forced her into survival mode. But she had survived it all and grown stronger and wiser.

Using the strong sewing scissors, Midlife Amy carefully worked to remove the duct tape. Lifting the grainy old fabric, she was relieved to find her gut instinct was correct once again. There really was another inner layer. And this fabric looked and felt very much like her old ski parka. But it wasn't white like that coat, the one her kids had affectionately called her "big, puffy jacket." Come to think of it, this fabric might've started out white. But in its current state, it was hard to tell.

Peering closely, she realized scraps of material were sewn in various places across the jacket fabric. But it was the words sewn onto the scraps that made her stop and drop the scissors: "responsibility," "expectation," "obligation," and "rejection." *You've got to be kidding me...*

Again using her scissors, she pulled the thread that attached one of the scraps to the jacket lining. Underneath a "responsibility" scrap, she discovered a rather large tear in the fabric. She pulled the thread on another scrap...and another...and each one covered a tear in the fabric. She had always been impressed with her Cape, but this discovery made it seem even more powerful.

Did my Cape attempt to repair itself each time it experienced a tear from pleasing others instead of myself? Each time I took on too many responsibilities and obligations? Gave too much power to expectations and rejections?

Grabbing the edge of this second layer of fabric, she realized that there was no additional trim. In fact, the edges were frayed and… *Could it be…?* The edges looked almost as if they'd been burned? *Of course, the edges are burnt and frayed,* she thought. This second inner lining absolutely resembled her life as Single Mom Amy, who attempted to soar while existing in a constant state of stress and burnout. The fabric's tears and burns were the results of her demands that the Cape adapt. Without regular care, she had just pushed through the pain and stress. *Isn't that what superheroes do?*

Curious as to what was holding it all together, she grabbed the frayed edges. Surprised again, she found a wire-like thread that seemed to zigzag around the bottom of the remaining fabric. This persistent thread seemed determined to keep the inner layers together. When she tried to pull some of the thread out with her scissors, it wouldn't budge.

Clearly, this was the heavy thread of survival that had kept her Cape together for so long. She sat staring in awe. Her Cape was far more powerful and capable than she had realized. And it was still holding itself together, despite her best efforts at neglect.

Discovering that the Cape did indeed have multiple inner layers, she felt even more hopeful. *Little Amy's original lining might be somewhere under all of the adapted survival.* Using grip strength, patience, and pliers, the wirelike thread from the edges released the parka fabric from what lay beneath it.

Midlife Amy gasped. *Bright and shiny blue, this third inner layer resembles the Cape's exterior!* But, right in the middle of this fabric, a bright-white *M* shone back at her. She could only laugh. *Totally Super Mommy!*

And to her surprise, this third new layer of fabric was covered with stickers. Yes, stickers! And on these stickers, she found the same words that were on the parka scraps: "responsibility," "expectation," "obligation," and "rejection." Curious, she peeled off one of the stickers, assuming they also covered tears in the lining's fabric. But to her surprise, she discovered a beautifully embroidered "curious" beneath the sticker. Lifting another sticker, she found "capable"; under another, "daring."

Shocked and ashamed, she wondered when the people-pleasing drivers had taken over her Cape. Finding words like "expectation" and "obligation" on two of the inner layers, she was saddened to realize how much of her life she had spent *trying* to please others, rather than fueling and satisfying her own curiosity.

And on this Super Mommy lining, the responsibility traits covered her original enthusiastic, natural way of viewing life. Yet she was relieved to see that traits like daring were still on this inner lining. They were simply covered up because she had refused to feel and accept her pain and disappointment because she felt unworthy of prioritizing her own desires.

At Amy's core, she had always been curious, capable, and daring; she was always willing to try something new and go off on an adventure. But as Super Mommy, she had allowed a need to care for and please others to dictate the Cape's focus and achievements.

She sat with these hard feelings of sadness, guilt, and shame…and eventual acceptance. Shame turned into self-compassion. Thinking of her younger selves, she reasoned that she had done her best to try and live her best life. Serious adulting had forced her to choose between her own desires and those of the people around her. Society had rewarded her for her mature, selfless choices. Yet Little Amy's authentic self was lost beneath the weight of serious adulting.

As she sat with the stickers in her hands, she felt really sad for her little self and for her adult friends. She knew this was likely a sad reality for most adults. They had done the best they could at the time, just as Amy had. But now she knew better. So she would try to do better.

Grasping the edges of the Super Mommy layer, she looked down and burst out laughing. It seemed that images of her children's achievements had attached themselves to the fabric's edge, as if they were a satin trim holding the fabric together. The trophies and ribbons reminded her of the T-shirt quilts she had made for her kids when they graduated from high school. She had saved special T-shirts from all of their soccer and baseball uniforms, special tournaments, and state championships. And she gifted the T-shirt quilts to her kids when they graduated from high school. Ironically, it seemed she enjoyed the quilts more than her kids did. *Perhaps they will appreciate them more after they have put a little distance between them and their youth?*

Staring at the satin trim of accomplishments, well, it made a lot of sense. Their successes and achievements, happiness and celebrations had truly felt as if they were her own parenting achievements as well. *Why should it surprise me that they are holding Super Mommy's Cape together?* Her kids were her purpose, her guiding North Star during that twenty-year season of her life.

And now, she had launched her baby birds. They had their own Capes of Courage and Capability. And it was time, once again, for Amy to be the star of her own story. In order to do that, she needed to uncover the core layer of this Cape.

It was underneath the Super Mommy fabric that she discovered a fourth layer of the Cape's inner lining. While it appeared to be a slightly shorter duplicate of the layer before, the only major difference was what lay in the middle of the fabric. Where the last layer featured the letter *M* for Mommy, this lining featured a giant white star.

It took Amy several moments of confusion before she understood its significance. When you consider the early-adulting season of her life, the star made perfect sense. During those younger versions of Amy—Sorority and London, Professional and Newlywed—she herself intentionally played the starring role in their stories.

And the star didn't symbolize an arrogance per se. Rather, Early Adulting Amy allowed her imagination, dreams, and self-actualization to take center stage while making choices during her pivotal moments. There were few plot twists for the Cape; it was a decade in which Amy was the leading lady.

And this lighter fabric seemed to allow for such a star's lifestyle. Beautiful and yet durable, this layer seemed to offer ease for someone who'd want to ignite her own magic. And while she didn't find any visible tears, she did notice some beautifully embroidered words across the fabric: "courage," "positivity," "kindness," and "drive." Just reading the words seemed to ignite a little glow of energy inside the Cape.

But the true magic on this lining? Gray stickers of depression lay to the side of her empowering traits like optimistic, free spirit, and dazzling. Rather than cover her authenticity, as in previous layers, they seemed to politely share the space—almost as if they were nodding respectfully to each other's capabilities and existence.

It appeared that Younger Amy who wore this version of the Cape had not yet let the negativity and heaviness of pleasing others cover her shiny authenticity. It would seem she had discovered the existence of these heavier parts of life, yet she had found a way for all of her emotions and characteristics to coexist on her Cape, as a normal mortal human would have. This duality in the Cape was beautiful; Younger Amy certainly was ahead of her time in finding such balance at a young age.

Younger Amy had not allowed life's struggles, disappointments, and rejections to keep her from being her authentically positive and capable self. She felt an immense sense of pride in her younger self...and yet sadness at the same time. She could see how her overachieving had led to Super Mommy and a desire to be everyone's hero except her own.

Feeling tremendous relief in discovering Younger Amy's Cape, she wondered if this freshly uncovered layer would enable Midlife Amy to activate the old magic. *Can I use it to channel the dazzling and daring leading lady?* She didn't have to be everyone's hero all the time.

Her hands touched the soft satin ribbon on the edge of the inner fabric. Lowering her readers off her nose for a closer look, she read the following words printed on the ribbon: "You can be so much more," "Win that award," "Work on that serve," "Work harder," "Don't disappoint them," "You're not enough," "Don't quit." Immediately, she recognized the words. They consisted of phrases from her own self-talk, Young Adult Amy's own words, and those from others who had influenced her Cape. This string reflected the voices of her confident younger self and her tough, challenging inner critic.

This underlying ribbon of perfectionism and the people-pleasing thread had both weighed down the Cape's edges and held the Cape together for all of these years. Once again, duality was alive and well on the Cape.

Shocked, she held the ribbon in her hands, and cried for each of her younger selves. They had done such a great job of navigating the good and bad influences while trying their best to retain their authenticity. *But how could they have known the plot twists that lay ahead? They couldn't have imagined what was coming down the road. And even if they had, how could they have reacted any differently?*

The younger Amys had always enjoyed a lifelong confidence in their capabilities. And while they had been so close to loving themselves, the inner critic had prevailed. The words, opinions, and expectations of others had become permanent additions to the Cape.

No wonder the Cape felt so heavy… No wonder it was so very hard to keep flying.

With the four inner layers removed, the Cape certainly felt much, much lighter. And Midlife Amy felt very inspired to live like Little Amy. She recognized the determination of her younger selves; when she added Midlife Amy's wisdom to that, she felt hopeful that, wearing this refreshed Cape, she might actually be able to live like the star of her upcoming story, of the seasons and episodes of her life yet to be written.

Gathering the worn, tattered layers of lining that no longer served her, she carried them out to the garbage can. The relentless threads of survival and people-pleasing were next, along with the ribbon of criticism—it no longer served her either. Those voices had gotten her this far, but she had nothing left to prove to anyone but herself.

She reinforced the trim with a light, stretchy fabric that felt like her yoga pants. This refreshed inner lining would remind her to remain flexible while experiencing life. To be intentional in her reactions—especially to put on her own oxygen mask first. To serve the hero she wanted to be first, rather than start with the needs of others.

She added a ribbon of ambition—*Yes, you can!*—around the edge of the reassembled Cape. She had put her own career dreams on hold so many years before. *Perhaps it is time to take on a more senior role in my career? Prove to myself that I am capable of so much more. If not now, then when?*

Midlife Amy felt ready to wear her Cape once again. She was determined to soar for herself and for the dreams and curiosity of her younger selves. With great hope, she proudly tied the strings of the Cape around her neck. She was ready to focus on the what-ifs and embrace her fears. She knew better now. She would try to step out of her comfort zone. She would be curious once again.

It is my time to fly.

Chapter 18

The Test Flight

Confident in the self-reflections and lessons she had gained while examining the inner layers of her Cape, she found herself intentionally considering, *What does Little Amy need?*

With the weight of serious adulting and overachieving removed, she knew Little Amy would insist on a test flight soon. So she gladly tied the lighter Cape around her neck, ready to practice her new boundaries and self-care. And that meant channeling her younger selves.

There was nothing stopping this intentional practice in self-focus. Just that fall, her son successfully transferred to a new university. He was so much healthier and growing happier. Her daughter was plugging along in her own college and young-adulting journey. And Less Foggy Amy was practicing maintaining boundaries and continuing her journey of healing with regular therapy.

She made the very difficult decision to end the romantic relationship with her partner. She felt terrible pain and sadness, and she was fearful of a future alone. But with her babies living into their young-adulting chapters, it was time to do the same with her own new chapter.

Midlife Awakened Amy knew that no one was coming to save her. It had always been up to her to create the Cape's flight path. The open field and sky felt pretty scary. Unlike during her younger pivotal moments, at this age, she struggled with imagining any path in this world without her children living under her roof. And the term "empty nest" sounded sad and pitiful. The words made her feel that way—as if her life were over.

But as we know, Single Mommy was one of many different versions of Amy across her lifetime. And those other versions of her needed to wake up and take her fresh Cape for a spin. As with anything new she faced, Midlife Amy put on her student hat once again. She wanted to learn how to live into this new normal. She certainly wasn't the first parent to go through this change. She wondered, *How do others find a way to thrive without their baby birds at home?*

She remembered when her kids were little, and she discovered a trick to learning from her fellow-parent friends—those a chapter or two ahead of her, anyway. So she sought the wisdom of other empty nesters and found many—friends, neighbors, books, podcasts, social media. The modern-nest elders were suddenly everywhere she looked.

During her self-study, she encountered a phrase that would completely shift her entire perspective on this sad stage of life. One author used the term "bird launchers" to refer to empty nesters. *Bird launchers! What an amazing rebrand! Boy, do I love the sound of that.*

Yes, Midlife Amy had indeed successfully launched her baby birds. A devoted parent with an empty nest. Still worrying about them, but hoping she had equipped them to safely soar into lives filled with much happiness. With distance coaching from Mom and Dad, the birds were learning how to be adults. These early-adulting birds had their own lives to lives. Their Capes would continue to grow with their unique challenges and choices, which were not those of the bird launchers. They needed to be free to make mistakes, to fall off a branch a time or two.

But for someone who had parented for more than twenty years—often putting their children's needs ahead of their own—this was terribly scary. Giving up the illusion of control over your children's Capes and trusting them to fly safely? But yet still being available should they have a little crash? And finding a way to not sit by the phone just in case she was needed? It all took some getting used to as she tried to prioritize her own big-bird life.

While the nest might feel very quiet, comparatively, a bird launcher should be celebrated, not pitied. Revered for their wisdom and accomplishments. Treated as elders to be consulted with and observed for their ability to soar through this next stage of life.

Midlife Amy knew this to be true. It was time for her dreams. But she asked herself the scariest question, *Where do I begin?* She felt scared because she just didn't have the answer. She was still afraid to do something wrong.

Once she addressed that fear, she thought about what she would say to her own kids. But even better, these days, Amy's common response to fear was to think about Little Amy. *What would she do? What had she done when she felt afraid but tried "the thing" anyway?* Yes, well, she believed in the magic of her Cape and proceeded fearlessly. She tried. She understood that she might fail. But knew that if she did, she would learn.

And Midlife Amy was tired of feeling afraid, and even more tired of having to have all the answers. She was ready to learn. And that meant putting on her Cape of Courage and Capability and leaving her comfort zone. She had to trust that she would figure things out. And if she couldn't, she'd ask for help.

Bird Launcher Amy's fear stemmed from many unanswered questions: *Who am I now? What is my role in my children's lives? How do I still show my love for them? How do I help them to live their best lives? How do I support them without irritating them or getting in the way? How do I cook for one? What do I do with my time??*

And at the same time, she realized she had a desire to rekindle the dreams and ambitions of her younger selves. *Who do I want to be? What do I want to do? Where do I want to go next? Whom do I want to join me?*

The more that Bird Launcher Amy embarked on her mission to get to know Little Amy, the more her attention, slowly but surely, focused on herself instead of her kids. She channeled her younger selves, their fierce curiosity and courage. Their why-nots and what-ifs. She wanted to take smart risks and shake up the norm. She knew Future Amy was counting on her. And once she realized that, she used Future Amy as an important consideration in all of her tries.

With healthy baby birds launched, tentatively but flying, she decided to stretch her own wings. It was time to relaunch Mama Bird. She had been offered a senior leadership role at a start-up tech company. And, this time, she didn't want to turn it down. It was a big risk, leaving the comfort of her COVID work family. But the newly redesigned Cape was restless, bored, and ready for a test drive. She needed a challenge, and she thought, *Why Not? Let's fly! It's time to relaunch myself.*

And while she soared into the new job, new company, and new people with her classic optimism and vision of possibilities, the year proved to be one that would challenge all of the work she had put into refreshing her Cape. It would arguably be her biggest and most important test yet.

It sent her Cape flying backwards in a culture and environment so turbulent that Little Amy's desire to prove she was enough came seeping back into the seams. There was so much possibility for her success. But each time she completed a goal, the goalpost and game seemed to change. Leadership differed in what they thought her role should be. And, as an expert people pleaser, she found herself fragmented in trying to please everyone. She did everything for everyone except her. Sound familiar?

And before she knew it, she was caught up in trying to prove to a group of men that she deserved to be respected. Prove that she was more than enough and should be valued and supported. But she didn't trust them. And asking for their support felt as if she were requesting assistance, and she didn't want them to think she needed help.

But why shouldn't she expect her leaders to help her succeed? Why couldn't they clearly see how impossible it would be for her, or anyone, to succeed in that role with so many different expectations of her and her work? With so many different people's needs to please? Why wouldn't her leaders want to help, support, and ensure she had what she needed to be successful for the company?

She woke up one morning seven months in and looked in the mirror. She had no idea who the woman was looking back at her. The strain of months of sheer fear of failure, of no psychological safety or trust, of no consistent definition of success, of stress and toxicity reflected back.

She was a shell of her former self. She had no energy, had gained fifteen pounds, and did nothing every day but get up at the crack of dawn, pour coffee, and roll into her office. She attempted to advance her plans, only to be disregarded, deprioritized, and left with a loss of confidence and a distorted sense of reality.

After ten hours, she crawled out of the office at dinnertime, too tired to go to the gym. She walked the dog if she hadn't had a break to do so during the day. Then, she spent the evening inside her house, responding to work phone calls. Then she tried to fall asleep, woke up, and continued the robotic spiral. She was completely empty emotionally and terribly depressed.

She had almost thirty people counting on her leadership, while her own leaders offered no support, no leadership for her. And her servant leadership style, persona, and way of showing up lived in stark contrast to the fear-based leadership that dominated her environment. Expectations of her varied by the person, and there was absolutely no way for her to succeed, nor ever find a way to thrive. Somehow, once again, she had gotten caught up in the cycle of surviving. Trying to make it work. Trying all the way into sickness. And she couldn't trust anyone to help her.

Then, the week before her birthday, she received a letter in the mail, reminding her to schedule her annual mammogram. It had been five years since her breast-cancer diagnosis. Five YEARS. She had certainly lived a lot of life in that time. But in the past year, what kind of life had it been? She had promised herself, after her cancer, that she would never just live again as if she were merely surviving. She had spent far too many years doing so. *And, now, who knows how long I have to live?*

Launching herself meant doing whatever was needed to thrive. But in this new job, she never stood a chance. She kept thinking, *I can make it better.* She thought she had enough power with her newly redesigned Cape to do so. But she finally realized that this was not a fight she should have to fight. It wasn't hers to begin with. And she wasn't willing to fight it any longer. She would never win. And she needed to thrive.

With the looming threat of the five-year mammogram date on the calendar, she knew she needed help to make this scary change, to extract herself from the toxic survival situation. And she knew it wasn't going to come from anyone within the work environment. Summoning courage from the Cape, she asked her doctor for help in finding a therapist.

And her new mind coach was exactly what she needed. He helped her step out of her trying-to-please spiral. He observed that her Cape was on its way to an inevitable crash. He validated that she was living in a toxic relationship with her work. And then asked her, "Do you really need to prove yourself any further to them?"

What a great question! As she sat in awe, the realization was both shocking and calming. A bright light spread across her Cape. She realized that when she was trying to please those men, she was actually back to doing whatever it took to please another toxically masculine man who could never support her or give her what she needed to be successful. Someone like her father. And that, as she knew, was an exercise in futility.

Here she was, in her early fifties, a successful, confident woman who, in the face of danger and fear, had reverted to pleasing people. She wouldn't fight. She was tired of fighting. Her trauma response was to please. But she would never please everyone, and she knew that in her heart.

In fact, after all that she'd brought to the table, she realized that no one was pleasing *her*. She was not feeling respected or appreciated. *Why should I stay in a situation where people make me feel that way? What would I tell my children to do in a similar situation?* The answer—she would've made them leave ages ago. But the persistent, determined Little Amy was committed to figuring it out—she was determined to a fault. She absolutely hated to *quit*. She needed a better word.

When the therapist suggested that she was living in a toxic relationship with her work, and might possibly be staying for the "children" (her team), she realized that's exactly where her mind had been living. She felt as if her team "needed" her protection—that's what drove her Cape every single day. She couldn't protect Little Amy, but she could try to battle to protect her team.

But who is protecting me? Realizing that the answer was nobody, she knew then what she had to do. She absolutely hated to quit anything, but since no one else was coming to her aid, she must stand up for herself. "Quitting" was the word she hated most. *But why?*

And at that moment, she knew the answer. It all finally connected. If she hadn't searched for Little Amy, and gained the wisdom and perspective of her younger selves and their choices, she might've missed it. She now recognized clearly the reason she hated to quit…anything.

Isn't it likely that I associate quitting with my dad leaving our family to start a new one? He made me feel not enough?

Just like that, there it was. And in that moment, she uncovered a driving force behind her behavior for all of these many years. She did not want to live like her father. Did not want to make anyone feel the way he had made her feel. And yet she had been working for people who reminded her exactly of him. And she had been driven to prove them wrong.

She had chosen to fight them in her own way: as the Overachiever Aim, who was so deeply embedded in the Cape's fabric that she could not be removed, no matter how hard she tried. It was her survival instinct. She thought her layers of capability were her advantage, but it was too deeply married to the tendency to overachieve. If she didn't do something soon, she knew a loud crash landing was imminent.

And it took one awful meeting to finally cause her to lose the last shred of patience and snap. It was the proverbial straw that broke the camel's back. She had finally had enough. She allowed her anger to take over and force the decision. She said no to the toxic environment. To leaders who lead with fear, disrespect, condescension, and profit before people. They had chipped away at her confidence. Challenged her need to please and prove them wrong… just as her father did for so many years. But she had nothing left to prove. It wasn't quitting. It was choosing herself. She was enough, but her job was not.

And once she left the toxic environment, she removed her armor. She allowed herself to feel the negative feelings, no matter how much they hurt. She felt the pain, disappointment, sadness, and frustration. She was determined to process her survival emotions. She had no room to carry the toxicity or negativity on her Cape. They didn't deserve any space on her Cape—they did not deserve her. And she had no desire for another heavy inner lining on the Cape!

And once she began to process the negative feelings, validating why she felt the way she did, she began to remember who she was. The optimistic, resilient, and glass-half-full girl picked herself up, brushed off the stupidity and the pain of the last experience, and moved on. Just as she had always done.

But, this time, she felt the strongest desire and intention she'd ever felt to live as her most authentic self. This test flight was not something to be regretted. She'd wondered if she could do it, and she did. Given a better environment, she might've thrived. She probably still could in a different environment.

But the test flight released something so powerful on her Cape. It released the lifelong desire—the survival instinct—to prove herself. For so many darn years, she had given her magic to others, rather than enjoy life for herself. She was done with giving away her power. She would not compromise her values and purpose for people who, and environments that, lived counter to her principles. She had nothing left to prove to anyone else. But she had everything to prove to Little Amy, Teen Amy, Sorority Girl, Super Mom, Bird Launcher, and every other version of her. She had the rest of her life to live for all of them.

But, first, she needed to heal. She needed to spend time apologizing to her younger selves and allowing them all to heal.

Chapter 19

The Sabbatical

For the first time in her adulting life, she took a professional break. She wasn't taking off the Cape—just hanging up the blazer for a while. She announced this change to her professional network, calling it a sabbatical. The outpouring of support completely stunned her. Her former colleagues applauded her decision. They acknowledged the long haul of major plot twists and life events she had pushed through. They cheered and expressed joy for her. She had not realized she needed the reinforcement, but it sure felt great.

She had been a planner for as long as she could remember, lining up one goal after another. But for once in her life, she had no idea what she was going to do next. For once in her life, she didn't have a plan. For once in her life, she listened to the voices of her younger selves. And they wanted her to rest, process, feel, and heal. And at the same time, they wanted her to play. Choose joy and wonder over obligation and pleasing everyone but herself.

She chose to spend her time thinking about her little selves, once again. Accessing those Wonder Woman episodes in which she had defied the odds and made shit happen all by herself. But, this time, she watched through the lens of the educated Older Amy's mind. The constant stress and strain on her Cape had so obviously impacted the health of her body.

Younger Amy always knew there had to be a mind-body connection—her theories were virtually tested on herself. She attempted to adopt wellness practices and make changes, but she had never quite been able to release the perfectionism or lack of self-worth that lined her Cape.

Being in a constant state of survival was not how she wanted to live her future. And something continued to nag at her. She had believed that the original purpose of the Cape was to give Amy the courage to try new things, explore the world, imagine and make those dreams a reality. The Cape helped support her curiosity, helped her build the confidence to learn and grow. *But hadn't Little Amy first discovered her Cape during a time of trauma? Had it been there before, but I just hadn't really seen it?* She was struggling to connect the dots.

There was one person who might be able to help. She chose to have another conversation with her mom. She wanted to talk about her seventh birthday—the day the man came into their home. She could picture the events that unfolded as if they had happened last month. But she wanted to hear her mother tell the story.

So it was many, many years after the home invasion that Older Amy learned that Little Amy, in fact, had not saved the day on her seventh birthday. The hero's story she had told herself for forty years was not actually quite true.

According to her mom, she had indeed run to the garage to get help from the landscaper. And her running out of the house did indeed scare the intruder into leaving. Mom called the police when the intruder left. Help arrived shortly afterwards.

But it turns out that Little Amy had not reached Charles, the landscaper, to ask for her help. She was actually found hiding in the garage behind her dad's golf cart. She was only seven-years-old. *How could she actually be a Wonder Woman?*

Older Amy sat silently in shock as she processed her mother's memory of the story. It sure made a lot more sense than the superhero episode Amy had been playing in her head for decades. *Does this mean I have been living a lie all these years? I'm really not all that special, after all.*

Given these details, one might wonder what would have happened to Little Amy had she learned, at age seven, that she indeed had not been the one to get help. That the adults in her life had actually taken care of her.

It is quite likely that Little Amy would've still always believed that she wore a Cape of Capability. She was a child with an easy joy, curiosity, and wonder about the world. Her magical spirit, confidence, and optimism probably would've activated her Cape, regardless, to encourage her to try whatever her imaginations and dreams required.

But since her seventh birthday, she had grown up believing that her Cape was responsible for making her a hero for other people. If she had not experienced the trauma that resulted in her seeing the Cape after that very, very scary day, what would Little Amy's life have been like today? For her entire life, would she have carried the burden of pleasing people, of overachieving, and of striving for perfection?

Likely. Her dad was who he was, intruder or not. And there were elements to her natural personality that were inclined to please others—for example, she was naturally a helper. But if the traumatic experience occurred today, a mental health professional would very likely support Amy in processing and healing from the experience.

It turns out that her mom had, indeed, wanted her to see a mental health professional right after the home invasion, but doctors told her no. They didn't think she should bring up the incident unless Amy did. They assured her that Little Amy would forget about it. And given her naturally happy personality, she did appear to be fine and unaffected by the traumatic events.

If she had been taken to a therapist to talk through the events, she might've realized that it wasn't her fault (or her mom's) that her mom didn't look out the window to see who it was. That the man had simply made a very bad choice. That it wasn't her job to protect her mom.

She should've been allowed to talk about the home invasion and feel all of the emotions she was experiencing after the terrifying experience. And be assured that she was okay. That she was enough. That adults were able to help and protect her, and she could go on growing up as a carefree child. But once trauma breaks a person's veil of safety and sense of security, the scars naturally remain.

If she would've gotten help to process all that she was carrying in her mind, she might have realized that her shiny blue Cape was not, in fact, actually real. In her mind, she was Wonder Woman, and she wore a Cape of Courage and Capability. But, of course, in reality, she was just a mere mortal with no actual superhuman powers. And since she didn't get help with processing the trauma, her seven-year-old mind attached itself to her Cape and the superhero story. Little Amy and the Cape grew up together, taking the hero's path—its ups and its downs.

As an adult, speaking with her mother about the event was such a critical plot twist for Midlife Amy. There it was, revealed—the lifelong challenge she felt as a naturally happy, fearless, and optimistic girl living side by side with the self-inflicted burden of being a hero to everyone but herself.

She always felt dumbfounded when people said, "You know, not everyone would be able to do what you've done."

Confused, she routinely replied, "Of course, they would if they had to." But now she realized that not everyone believed they had to save the day.

It was a lot... Older Amy sat with this understanding for a long time. It explained so much. And so she gave the Cape a big, long hug and soaked the fabric with her tears. And when she finished the healthy cry, she felt a lightness that can best be described as a long sigh of relief. And the Cape, too, relaxed...finally.

The sabbatical proved to be a huge pivotal moment, probably the biggest in Amy's life. The search for Little Amy revealed some fascinating truths and the true power of Amy's imagination.

The notion of a self-fulling prophecy felt very clear in Amy's situation. She had thought she needed to be a hero, and so she acted like one. She became a hero in her mind, in her actions and resilience, and in her determination and fierceness.

But Little Amy had always believed she *could* be a hero. It wasn't until her seventh birthday that the Cape's actions became a *should*—an *obligation* to use her superpowers. Little Amy channeled her Cape to enable her imagination, her curiosity, and her dreams. The Cape reminded her of her confidence and capabilities...and rewarded her tries. It was when she felt the weight of being a Little Adult that the responsibilities and obligations of being a hero crept to the forefront of her Cape. The *shoulds* surpassed the *coulds*, the *surviving* surpassed the *thriving*. She spent decades pleasing other people and raising little people by herself. She didn't have the time or energy for imagining how she herself could thrive. She wore the Cape—she was a hero, dammit.

During her sabbatical, she dug deep into reviewing the episodes of her hero's journey—those pivotal life moments and plot twists. She revisited the Cape and her younger selves and was fascinated to see them through the lens of her older, wiser, more compassionate self. *Why did I push myself so hard? Why did I care so much more about other people's reactions than my own?*

She knew things needed to change. She needed to learn to love herself: To put herself first. To remember what it was like to imagine and dream without the fear of failure or the heavy weight of responsibility. It was beyond time to let go of the old Responsibility Cape—let go of surviving adult life events and carrying the weight of it alone.

Armed with a new clarity about the past, she remembered who she was at her core. And now that her baby birds had launched, there was so much that she didn't need to carry anymore. She didn't have to wear her armor every day just in case it was needed. But she was afraid.

Well, of course, she was. She didn't know what she was supposed to do next. She loved the freedom of her sabbatical—it was like a test drive of her future retirement life. But her savings were dwindling as her energy and passion returned.

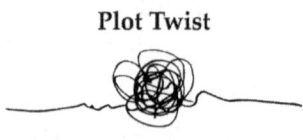

Plot Twist

Here she sat, in a pivotal moment so similar to pre-London Amy. Once again, she had few obligations, and a big wide world was open before her. *So what do I want to be when I grow up? What do I want to do with the rest of my life?*

She had no clue, but she did have an idea about where to start. She walked into her home office and sat on the couch. She had tried a range of different occupations during her career—several the result of plot twists she had survived. As she looked around the room, she realized it was all in the abyss of her office—the relics of Achiever Amy's life. This last tangible space contained the artifacts of her younger selves. She had procrastinated about addressing, embracing, and mending these remains during the sabbatical. But it was time. *Is the answer here?*

She rolled up the shades on the windows, turned on her old CD player, and popped in the Backstreet Boys' *Millennium* CD—her old cleaning inspiration. AC/DC and Metallica would come next, then maybe a little Garth Brooks. It was time to clean out and reorganize her office sanctuary. Time to come face-to-face with the past in order to figure out the future.

She began with the giant bookcase. Each shelf was crammed with books spanning the course of her life. Everything from her first published poems, *Breezes from Diablo*, to her high school copy of *The Adventures of Tom Sawyer*, her college communications textbooks, and those she used to teach communications. Countless books on teaching elementary school, leadership, her high school yearbooks, parenting, sales and customer success, and even a collection of her great-grandmother's cookbooks. The collections revealed her range of careers and interests. And, of course, her love of reading.

She began pulling the books down and creating piles on the floor based on topics. After dusting off the shelves, she remembered another box of books in her closet. She dragged it out, dusted it off, and dug in. Opening the box, the first thing she saw was her old dictionary. It didn't really fit into any of the piles, but if she had to choose, she'd put it with her teaching books. Teacher Amy had used her personal dictionary to teach vocabulary to her fifth-grade students. This box was filled with her favorite personal books, taken off a shelf in her classroom on her last day.

The Random House College Dictionary – a gift on Amy's thirteenth birthday, June 1984.

With Teacher Amy in mind, she picked up the large red *Random House College Dictionary* and opened the cover. She had completely forgotten… There, written on the inside page, was the inscription from her stepmother:

June 19, 1984 (her 13th birthday)
Amy,
Hope this will help you to develop your writing talent.
With Much Love,
Charlie

Her "writing talent"—even her stepmom had known how much Young Amy wanted to be a writer. She smiled, holding the dictionary to her chest. It was her big, crazy, audacious dream.

For as long as she could remember, she could visualize walking into a bookstore, approaching the display of new books, and seeing it. Her book, staring back at her. She couldn't go into a bookstore without smiling at that silly old dream…every single time.

She pulled the rest of the beloved books out of the box and got to work assigning them space on the bookshelves. Bookcase finished, she stumbled across another box; this one looked even older. Opening the top, she discovered it was filled with Little Amy's prized relics: trophies, track ribbons, certificates of achievement, and awards. At the bottom, she found high school and college photos. She smiled, looking at Teen Amy and Sorority Aim. Her mind drifted back vividly to the memories of the sorority formal photos, her college dorm room, her friends, and living the time of her life.

She pulled her favorite trophies and photos out of the box, and decorated her desk with the memories. She would sit with these relics of her younger self and see what inspiration they brought to Future Amy. What had she forgotten? What brought her joy? What path had she not taken that she just might revisit now?

Lost in the world of her younger selves, the ring of her cell phone made her jump. She looked down to see her son was calling. It was the middle of the afternoon on a Wednesday. An old fear brought a sharp clutch to her stomach. He had not sent a text message. He was calling her.

Cautiously, after holding her breath for a second, she answered the call, "Hi, sweetie, are you okay?"

"Hi, Mom. Yeah, I'm okay. But I hurt my back."

She heard the calm voice of a twenty-year-old young man, yet the tone she recalled was that of her sweet nine-year-old telling her about a boo-boo. Her beloved college boy was living on his new campus. Juggling a crazy life on the rowing team with a huge course load, work in a research lab, and work in an autistic-behavior clinic. His schedule was nuts, but he was doing all the things he had wanted to try, and he was thriving.

Why had he called her that afternoon? He had hurt his back and wanted to tell his mom. He pulled a muscle trying to be the hero and row in a different seat, on the other side of the boat. Definitely her child.

"I'm so sorry to hear that. But I bet you know how to take care of it, huh?"

"Yeah, I'm doing icing, took some Motrin, and stretching."

"That's my boy. Well done. Do you want some money to get a massage?"

He laughed. "No, thanks! You give me enough money!"

He was fine. He was healthy, and he was safe. He was taking care of himself in the ways she had taught him. He was living his early-adulting life, and he was crushing it.

And then, her sweet boy proceeded to talk about all the things going on in his college life. It was a rare chance to catch a glimpse into his world…in the middle of the week. To learn about the normal college things he'd been doing, picturing him on campus with the sounds of other college kids' voices in the background. She typically hung on every single bit of news that he wanted to share—appreciation for "normalcy" would never be lost on her again.

But on this day, while Momma Amy was certainly listening, she was oddly distracted. She couldn't tear her eyes away from the photos in front of her. The scenes from *her* younger life allowed her to relive the joy and laughter of her college life—moments that Sorority Aim hadn't seen coming but loved. Suddenly, she realized that she had barely heard a word of what her son was telling her.

At first, she felt awful and fairly guilty—she was always so grateful for this precious time. But then, she realized *he* had interrupted *her*. While grateful that her son had called, she had not been sitting around waiting to hear from him. She had been busy finding Little Amy and getting reacquainted with her. Most importantly, she felt inspired to start living life as Little Amy had.

This bird launcher wasn't going to live only through her children's experiences. While she adored her children and looked forward to their calls and time spent with them, Midlife Amy was determined to launch her future self. Future Amy would continue to make her own memories, doing things that brought her joy, growth, laughter, challenge, disappointment, resilience, wonder, and love. She was going to live her life for herself. Being a mom was just one incredible part of who she was…but it was not everything.

And it was at that moment—well, after ending the call with her son—that she knew what she wanted. What she needed. In order to grow into her future self.

She wanted to feel like Little Amy, who was crushing life before her seventh birthday. The one who felt confident, courageous, and capable. The girl who boarded a plane to London at the age of twenty-three years old to live her best life. The one who flew through life embracing the what-ifs and why-nots. The one who responded to a challenge with, "I *know* I could do that!"

While she knew that her Cape wasn't actually real, her younger selves didn't know that. And if she was going to live like them, she was going to have to try hard to believe in Little Amy's Cape. And it started with believing in magic…her magic.

Chapter 20

New Habits

During her inspection of the old Cape's layers, she had pulled out the thread of people-pleasing, along with the inner layers that no longer served her and only added weight. Yet during the test flight, she realized that an expert level of people-pleasing thread had returned to the trim of her Cape. *What made it return?*

While living into her big leadership role, she had challenged her Cape with an advanced level of responsibilities and obligations. Early on, she felt capable and confident. Before she realized what happened, the thread of people-pleasing had taken over her Cape. And by the time she realized it, it was too late. The toxic situation and environment would never enable her Cape to survive. *Why did I push myself to stay? Why didn't I listen to my gut?*

The duality of the Cape

First, a healthy level of people-pleasing can play a critical role in the Cape's success. You can digest positive or constructive feedback to learn and grow. A growth mindset can be very healthy and can soar through the Cape.

However, at what point does an environment become toxic? Where does the need to please others get in the way of your ability to accomplish your own goals and pursue your dreams? If the environment you're trying to soar in can't support your magic, and it forces you to question your value, you need to find a different environment.

During her sabbatical, Midlife Amy noodled on this duality and tried to figure out how she could find a way to *try* while also respecting her *knowing*. And, if needed, how could she navigate her magic in the face of an unhealthy environment.

One day, while she was out on a run, an idea came to her. *Could it be that simple? What if the magic of her Cape could be ignited and sustained with a simple daily habit that was mindful—for example, brushing her teeth each day?*

What if, each morning and night, she took the time to examine her Cape to make sure the people-pleasing thread had not reappeared? And if it had, she could discover the root cause by examining the events of that day. Catch the damage before it spread over the Cape's inner lining?

Could it really be as easy as making daily Cape care a priority habit? Why hadn't she learned this before? Why had no one told her it wasn't selfish, but critical, to take care of her own mental health? As with cleaning and flossing for healthy teeth, you should take on daily habits to maintain a healthy Cape.

Rather than get frustrated, Sabbatical Amy's mind was clear enough to offer compassion to her Cape and understanding to herself. *Well, of course, the people-pleasing returned during the test flight!*

When faced with choices, Older Amy's were conditioned to triage the scariest and hardest things to manage. Please others before herself. Put herself last. And she did. And then, survive the Cape's crash landing.

Could Future Amy learn to live differently? Approach life with less self-sacrifice and more self-care? Live life with less self-criticism and more self-love, similar to how my younger selves lived?

She felt a palpable sense of hope. She knew it would take living like her younger selves to develop some new habits. Sure, she had been equipped to soar when she was young and wore a lighter Cape. But Older Amy believed she could soar even farther with her healthier, wiser, more seasoned mind. Most old dogs couldn't learn new tricks... but she had a Cape. And she wasn't a dog. She was Amy Sue Agnew Irvine, and she was going to finally learn how to take care of her Cape.

She knew she'd likely always tend to people-please and have to remove that thread when it returned—that was just a part of who she was. *But what can I control?* She could live intentionally to avoid triggering the need for it to appear. She could live and work within an environment that supported a healthy Cape. Yes, she absolutely could control and choose her environment—one that encouraged her to be the Amy she wanted to be, not who someone thought she could be.

She remembered that Little Amy had always wanted to be able to do and solve everything on her own. But no one had told her that it was an impossible feat for any human being. Super Mommy was so used to being a human *doing*, that she had forgotten how to be a human *being*. And Single Survival Mom thought she had to carry the weight of the world on her shoulders, all by herself.

But just because she *could* do things, didn't mean she *should. Why did it take me so long to realize that when something is too heavy, I should ask for help to carry it? Or just put the darn thing down!*

And none of the younger Amys had learned how to care for their Capes. Not even Midlife Amy. In fact, the test flight had left her body and mind in a state of serious neglect.

The sabbatical certainly provided Amy with the time and space to reflect and heal. Nearly a year without achievements had helped the thread of perfectionism to lie dormant. But what would happen when she stepped out of the bubble of healing and attempted to fly once again? She would need to make her self-care habits permanent.

Each morning, she imagined holding the Cape in her hands, searching for any tears, stickiness, or return of the threads of people-pleasing and perfectionism. One day, she found herself with lots of remorse about her last job. She found herself reliving situations she thought she could have handled differently. *Why did I stay so long and put up with so much disrespect?*

So much shame tried to penetrate the Cape's linings. While these thoughts were certainly natural to her processing and healing, she didn't want them to stay on the Cape. Grabbing her scissors, she got to work, pulling out the self-defeating thread on the Cape's inner lining.

Suddenly, within three pulls, she realized that there was something else attached. There was one more inner layer of shiny blue fabric—not nylon, but satin. She worked faster around the edge, and when she lifted the fabric, she cried very happy tears as she stared in disbelief at what was in the center of the Cape. There it was—the original inner layer of Little Amy's Cape. How could she be certain? Instead of a letter *M* or a white star in the center, she found a cursive letter *A*. And the thread attaching the *A* to the fabric? Well, it shone like diamonds...and looked magical.

The Cape's original satin lining was soft and shorter than the other layers of the Cape. Yes, this last layer was indeed Little Amy's original Cape. She sat stunned. If she hadn't been practicing her new habit of daily Cape care, she might never have found it.

And while she loved Little Amy's *A* in the center, it was the smaller words sewn around the bottom edge of the lining that made her cry. They seemed to be embroidered in her mom's beautiful cursive handwriting: "imagination," "dreams," "positivity," "joyful," "friendly," "playful," "curious," "creative," "athletic," "smart," "competitive," "kind," and "love."

She stared in awe—her original hero's Cape of Courage and Capability. These distinctly Little Amy traits had been there all along. Just covered by the inner layers of survival—the pain, fear, responsibility and obligations, people-pleasing, and seeking the approval of others, instead her own.

She knew, without a doubt, that Future Amy wanted and needed these natural, authentic traits to take front and center in her life. Of course, along with some of Older Amy's wisdom, skills, and experiences. But only those that served her future selves.

She sat with pride, smiling at the descriptions of her core little self. And with a sigh, she knew for certain that she was more than enough. She always had been. She had nothing left to prove to anyone but herself.

The love and care she had been giving to herself during the sabbatical clearly seemed to be igniting a sense of magic on the Cape. Every time she did something to take care of herself, she felt a sizzle of gratitude from the Cape.

The most powerful lesson learned during the Cape's test drive and her sabbatical journey? It didn't matter what she did to refresh the Cape if she didn't take care of it on a regular basis. And she needed to establish some requirements for a healthy Cape:

- Remain lightweight yet flexible to grow with Future Amy
- Continue with what is needed to pursue her dreams, especially to learn
- Harness the power of the confidence gained through life experiences
- Sustain a magical trim that reminds her she is the hero of her own story
- Remind her about her magical power to choose joy over fear, curiosity over stress, what-ifs over doubt, sunshine over gray

This lighter, leaner, and well-respected Cape would remind her to listen to and take care of herself first. When presented with an ask or a challenge, it will ask, *Can we or should we?* And that will trigger her knowing, her gut instinct, if she isn't sure.

It will remind her of who she is at her core, in case she dares to doubt. Courageous, daring, resilient, capable, joyful, wise, creative, compassionate, curious, helpful, driven, persistent, empathetic, and, yes, responsible.

And as she imagined this new Cape, an old photograph popped into her mind. It was a photo of her at a time in her life when everything and anything felt possible with her Cape.

Amy Sue Agnew, Acalanes High School, Lafayette, California, Spring 1982.

In the photo, she is running around the track with a huge smile on her face. You can almost feel her joy.

Based on the photo's location, it was clearly track-and-field season. Yet this was a time when she was juggling multiple sports, and she was wearing her competitive-soccer-team sweat suit. On the jacket, her mom had sewn patches. Not due to tears in the jacket's fabric, but to represent the many different soccer tournaments she participated in while playing on that team.

Wait a minute! The patches...They gave her an idea! What if I can do the same thing with my Cape? What if, on the inner layer of my Cape, I sew tiny patches that represent my courageous moments? Patches that will trigger memories of when in the past I tried and succeeded. When I persevered through fear and demonstrated courage in the face of fear and failure. Prevailed through punishing plot twists that activated my courage and determination. And remind me to be my own hero.

Could those patches serve as reminders of my confidence and capabilities when my future selves are afraid? Like episodes from the Story of Amy. *Could they confidently remind me that I am already a hero? That nothing should ever stop me from trying to realize my imaginings or dreams?*

These courage and capability patches would activate little sections of her memory so that she could draw upon what she needed, depending on the type of attempt or fear she was facing. They would help her soar with confidence when living the different roles that she played in life: Momma Amy, Professional Amy, Athlete Amy, Adventure Amy, Writer Amy, Friend Amy, Daughter Amy, Sister Amy, Auntie Amy... You get the idea.

The athlete patch would activate courage when she wanted to try a new sport, learn to surf, or train for another half-marathon. Or she could draw from her professional-skills patch when she was ready to end her sabbatical. The patches would activate her confidence and courage to try new things and believe in her capabilities. The more she lived life wearing her Cape, the more the power of the patches would grow. The more she dared, tried, failed, succeeded...

With this vision of her Cape in mind—Future Amy living as her most authentic self—she got to work adding the confidence patches. She selected different types of fabric to represent her determination, capability, and confidence. The special thread that would be woven throughout—her relentless optimism.

Restitching the updated Cape took a lot of time and patience. Just like her sabbatical, she didn't want to rush it, as she was still learning what she wanted to be intentional and what her next chapter would look like. And she reminded herself daily that the Cape needed to stay light and flexible enough to change and age with older Future Amy. She left room for new patches to be added—new journeys and experiences. And she felt inspired, peaceful, and more hopeful than she had in a very long time.

She had once used a Cape to be the hero of her own story. And that often meant using it to help others. But that's what made her, well, Amy. She loved helping others. But after finding her little selves, she knew she'd never again forget to put herself first and foremost.

While people might not have seen her Cape, they had seen the choices she had made and the actions she had taken. The smile she wore to tell everyone she was okay, even on the days she wasn't. But she wasn't going to do that anymore. Her smile had become the Cape people saw. But the real Cape, well, it was her mind, of course.

She felt, once again, a great determination to soar—to live a life of learning and taking chances. This time, she was not afraid to tear her Cape or fail. She knew she was capable of repairing any damage. She realized her mind was growing strong yet again. Taking off the Cape had worked. She was able to reset with the help of her little selves.

The strength of her new Cape truly reflected the strength of Amy's mindset—little, teen, and older Amys, all together. In reimagining her Cape to compartmentalize her capabilities, she had healed her mind. And her body responded favorably.

She knew life would continue to present plot twists, and she would always have choices to make during pivotal moments and plot twists. But she felt well-equipped to handle whatever came her way. And she knew, if she needed to, she could access her kryptonite: she could always ask for help.

Suddenly, "kryptonite" didn't seem like a fitting word anymore. She had thought asking for help took away her superpowers, made her less of a hero in her Cape. But, truly, moving forward, asking for help deserved to be celebrated—it was a superpower in itself.

With a clear mind, her imagination returned—her creativity and Authentically Amy voice was back. And she found that it had a lot to say. Sabbatical Amy returned to her journaling, and her voice came out loud and clear. Her imagination felt limitless. Everything in life felt clearer without the extreme heaviness she had carried for far too long.

And every Amy inside of her wanted to have fun, explore life, find joy and purpose. She didn't want to feel held back by fear. And in order to really understand what made her happy, she needed to do things by herself. Find out what made Amy happy—not her kids, her partner, her mom, her brother, her friends.

When had she become afraid to do things without a friend or a romantic partner? Wasn't she the girl who had moved to London all by herself? Well, yes, she was. In fact, why couldn't she channel her fearless twenty-three-year-old self?

She started slowly. There was a movie she wanted to see, kind of last minute…so she bought one ticket and went. She loved it. She wanted to watch football at a sports bar…so she put on her favorite jersey, sat down at the bar, and watched the game…and made friends. She wanted to go for a hike…so she went. You get the picture. She was not going to be afraid of being on her own.

What would people think if she was by herself? Well, it turns out, people thought she was pretty badass and fearless. And they were inspired to try doing things by themselves, too.

She could've asked several friends to go with her, but she decided to check off a bucket-list item all by herself. Well, that is, with the encouragement of a dear bestie. She bought a single ticket on the floor to see the artist Pink in concert, all by herself just hours before the show. It was one of the most memorable and joyful experiences of her life. And she would have missed it if she hadn't acted fearlessly.

Fear would no longer stop *this* Amy. She even volunteered to support the swim portion of the California Ironman race. With the encouragement of another friend, she spent hours on her stand-up paddleboard in the middle of a large river, paddling up stream, guiding and supporting the swimmers. It was one of the coolest experiences of her life. She even helped one man all the way to the swim finish. And, again, she almost missed it… but she didn't.

She sewed new experience patches onto her Cape, and she couldn't wait to add more. With each fearless try and return to play, she remembered one of her greatest loves—something she had done for nearly fifty years. She wanted to dance again.

At first, it was taking a Zumba class once a week. Then she found a dance-party class with hip-hop, disco, salsa, and line dancing. Looking at the mirror in that dance studio, she saw herself! The younger Amys—both Little and Teen Amy, College Aim, London Aim. They were smiling, laughing, and felt totally alive. And so did Midlife Amy.

And what about her fear of doing anything alone? Well, she discovered that she was never really alone. There were always people around her, and she had always loved making new friends.

When she introduced herself to new people, she found a voice coming out of her mouth that she had not heard in quite some time. The carefree laughter of Sorority Aim and the sassiness of London Aim. And, more importantly, she was learning how to be by herself—to actually enjoy her own company.

And the more she tried on her own, the stronger she felt. She discovered that she actually enjoyed herself. It dawned on her why she had avoided herself for so long. When she sat with the memories of her younger selves, looking within with compassion and understanding, she found she no longer was quite so very mean to herself. She started to remember who she was, and the other Amys began to return to the forefront of her mind. And how could she love them without loving herself as she was today?

Part 5 ~ Future Me

Chapter 21

The Reentry

The more inspiration Midlife Amy felt from her younger selves, the more she wrote. And the more she wrote, the more she learned about herself. You probably know where this is going…

The more she learned about herself, well, the more she loved herself. And when you love yourself, it's a lot harder to be mean to yourself. She began to treat herself the way she wanted her kids to treat themselves. The way she would want anyone to treat themselves. She had always been compassionate and empathetic with others—why not with herself? She knew she was worthy. She was enough just as she was right then and there.

But despite all the work that she put into her healing and the redesign of her Cape, Midlife Amy still did not feel satisfied. While her practice retirement was super awesome, she was not in a place financially to actually retire. She needed an income. And even if she won the lottery, she still wanted to live with purpose. She wanted to share her energy with the world.

As smart as she had been about her spending, her savings account was dwindling. It was time to reenter the workforce. But which of her numerous career paths did she want to pursue?

While there are lots of different ways to earn money, she just couldn't decide what to do next. And considering her desire to maintain a new daily Cape-care practice, she knew that her next job needed to provide that balance. She had spent so many years making the best of job situations in order to raise her kids. Now, it was time to prioritize her dreams—activate her magic.

She absolutely loved being a classroom teacher. And she still missed the job, even after twelve years. She felt the magic of the Cape activate with even the thought of creating her own classroom once again. Teaching ignited Amy's magic.

But K–12 classroom teachers were still vastly underpaid in the United States of America. The antiquated non-performance-based step-salary schedule system was not set up to compensate someone like her, someone who had taught college and performed learning-design and -facilitation roles for more than thirty years (with only two years of elementary-classroom teaching).

In order to be the hero of her own story, she needed an income that would provide financial security and an ability to save for her upcoming retirement, whenever that happened. A teacher's salary would not provide such stability, and she certainly wasn't going to look for a sugar daddy.

Similar to when she graduated from undergrad, the job market was horrible—so many people hunting for so few jobs. She began searching for positions at a mid-senior level in which she could coach and lead others, yet still be directly in the middle of the creative process. Less responsibility but more engagement on a team.

She wanted the ability to work hard during the daytime and then "shut off" the work to go play golf or pickleball, take a class at the gym, or go out to dinner with friends. She had no interest in evening calls or weekend emails from execs.

As the months passed, she wondered if achieving this balance might be hard to achieve. But she was determined. And it wasn't just her current self that she was thinking of—it was all of her younger selves and the future ones. They were counting on her.

With every job application she sent, the automated rejections arrived in her email inbox. At first, she laughed at them. Each of her previous jobs—every job since she was twenty-five years old, in fact—had come from referrals. She had never really applied and been rejected. Ever. So this was new. But she reasoned this was a healthy experience—a reminder of what being a job applicant felt like. As a leader, she would carry that empathy with her in the years to come.

But the rejections continued…and continued… and continued. Ever the optimist, she reasoned that they were redirections. But redirecting to what? Even when a job fell through, she realized she had been talking herself into the job because it was work that she knew and financial security.

Unfortunately, the rejections eventually began to take a serious toll on her confidence. Everything began to feel totally out of her control. If she hadn't been practicing her daily Cape care, she might not have recognized her dwindling confidence. Each day she woke up, it felt like Groundhog Day. The routine of checking her email to see if she had heard from the recruiter at the last job she had interviewed with. Nothing. With each email check, her confidence diminished a smidge more. And she learned that applying for a job without a referral was a total waste of energy.

At some point, she began to feel afraid. Her plan B had been to return to teaching—but now that was off the table. And as she looked at her resume, she felt frustrated that it didn't inspire a specific direction in which to focus. She began to write about her feelings and uncovered that she was feeling old and unwanted. Yet she knew how much she had to offer. It felt strangely similar to her desire to find a significant other, but she didn't know where to go to find him, either.

She had spent the past nine months learning how to feel enough as she was. She had worked hard to learn to love and respect herself. But the job-hunting process was testing her progress and requiring her to prove herself. And she was totally over having to do that.

As the weeks went by, the gray returned to her refreshed, formerly healthy Cape. But, this time, she could feel it. Since she had adopted her daily Cape-care regimen, she caught the gray. But at least she knew how to remove the gray—exercising and connecting with friends. She felt and talked about her feelings of rejection, frustration, and disappointment.

And when one particular final-round interview didn't yield the job, she felt devastated. At a loss for what to do next. She chose to sit with her feelings—let them out, process them, and let them go. She couldn't recognize how well she was taking care of herself, facing her feelings head-on, and not allowing them to attach to the Cape.

For Midlife Amy, this reentry felt like a total failure. *She* felt like a failure. She couldn't help but think, *Maybe I'm just expecting too much out of life?* She didn't know what to do, which was strange because she usually knew what to do. But she no longer had her plan B. What was plan C? She wanted someone to just tell her. *Why do I always have to do things by myself?* She sat in her pity party for quite a while. And she hated it.

But then she remembered what was missing. During the process of letting the rejections and disappointment chip away at her confidence, she had forgotten about her Cape. She had forgotten who she was. As her bestie always said, she was Amy Sue Agnew Irvine, dammit!

Amy's life journey had been filled with many turning points. These job rejections were just a part of the plot twist that she herself had activated. She had reclaimed her power and said, "Enough," when the environment was not serving her. *What would my younger selves tell me? Did I forget what living in the middle of a plot twist feels like?*

Of course, there was uncertainty! Of course, she felt scared! Of course, her magic seemed to be missing! Just because she was losing patience, that didn't mean her next chapter wasn't happening already. Maybe she wasn't supposed to focus on the job hunt itself. Her dear friend suggested that she write down all of the things she had done in the past nine months. Look at a photo of herself nine months ago. Recognize her healing, growth, and hard-earned peace.

While she didn't yet have the job for her next chapter, she had absolutely changed in so many wonderfully healthy ways. She just felt stuck in the mud of some really big changes and choices. Even though she was unsure about what to do for work, she couldn't help but be amazed at the changes she personally had made happen. She needed to celebrate her progress. She had begun to remember how to dream for herself, how to imagine future possibilities.

The fear she felt was natural. Of course, she was afraid. She was a human with some pretty awesome superpowers. While the sneaky gray kept trying to take over her Cape, her new daily habits were calling it what it was. She would not let depression and self-doubt sneak back in. It was time to shake off the sticky and believe in herself, yet again. It was time to activate the true Amy magic and fly fearlessly.

And since she hated a pity party, she decided to take her Cape and leave that sad state of rejection. She wasn't done with this Midlife Awakening. Yes, she was awake! But now she needed to live into the new Amy. She was attempting to reenter a world that had never really ignited the magic of her younger selves. The corporate jobs had been a means to an end—raising her children on her own. The money and corporate benefits finally brought a sense of financial security and breathing room to her single-parenting self.

But she no longer felt shackled by the burdens that had weighed down Single Mom. She didn't know what she was going to do next, but Future Amy needed her to imagine a new way of life without the heavy weight of achievement driving her every move. She didn't have to figure it all out—that was Future Amy's life to live.

She was capable of imagining an environment and lifestyle in which her future selves thrived with the core traits and capabilities of her younger selves. She needed to find Future Amy! And in order to do that, she needed to ignite the magic on her Cape.

She grabbed her laptop and headed to a quiet place. She needed to write.

Chapter 22

One Sunny Day on a Lake

The sun is shining brightly; it is the summer solstice. A light breeze and an occasional cluster of cumulus clouds keep the heat from forcing a sweat. The lake's water glistens, lapping against a paddleboard carrying two people and being launched from the shore.

"Hold on tight, Little Love!"

"But, Gramma, I want to try to paddle!"

"Yes, you can try, Love! But let's first get out into some calmer waters."

Her granddaughter smiles and relaxes, assured that she will indeed get a turn at trying to steer their vessel. She always gets to try new things with Gramma Amy—and sometimes the experiences are new for Gramma, too!

Gramma admitted that she was very afraid when she first learned to paddleboard. Scared to stand, afraid she'd fall in the water or hurt herself. But she taught Little Love that her Cape helps her try even when she feels afraid. In fact, she's already shown Little Love how to fall and safely get herself back up on the board.

Little Love believes that her Gramma is fearless. She wants to feel fearless, too. And learning how to fall and get back up gives her confidence that she can fly.

Marveling in her granddaughter's fearlessness, Gramma Amy's smile is a confident one. She knows what is likely about to happen, but she believes that Little Love is ready. She has witnessed the magic before, and she can't stop smiling in anticipation.

As she expertly paddles out towards the little island in the middle of the lake, her granddaughter leans back against her. The warmth of her little body brings a flood of love and gratitude. Gramma Amy recognizes, quite clearly, that she is living her dream—grateful for this life she intentionally created for herself. In this moment, she can't help but think back in time, marveling at the memory of a rather scary pivotal moment in a chapter of her life so many years before—the one she called her sabbatical. It was a time filled with so much uncertainty and intentional personal growth.

She had previously spent much of her adult life rushing through the pivotal moments, trying to come up with new plans. But during the sabbatical, she spent time in the liminal space—patiently sat within it. Tried, failed, and tried again to adopt new mindsets and habits that would support her desire to thrive. She chose to shift away from the need to have it all figured out. And shifted towards a desire and mindset to embrace life at a slower, more profound, and intentional pace.

But what if? What if she had not found the courage, patience, and faith in herself to exit the cycle of survival? After years of parenting as Super Mommy and Single

Surviving Mom, she had just needed to finally focus on herself. Put the oxygen mask on herself first.

If she had not embraced that critical pivotal moment in her midlife, what would she be doing today? Would she be physically capable of standing on the paddleboard at this older age? Would she have been intentional and committed to living like Little Amy? To infuse play and exercise into each and every day. Whether it was taking dance lessons or playing sports she had loved as Little Amy, accessing sources of joy that she could age with. And trying new activities that challenged her to learn and stretch, such as learning to surf and feeling, not numbing, the hard feelings. Would she have discovered that she had always been the hero of her own story?

Since that sabbatical, or what her son called her midlife gap year, she had become so laser-focused on living a life of thriving that she was able to forget about her finely sharpened survival tools and just breathe. To release the weight of having to be the one who saves the day. To let others step up and lead.

She had been able to let go of the parts of her Cape that no longer served her. She shifted her mindset and changed habits to practice daily Cape care. Began each day with positive inputs and intentions to relax and focus her mind. Finished the day with gratitude, imagining the possibilities for the next day.

Without all of those changes, would she have found a way to make her most audacious dream come true? The one that came with a feeling so overwhelmingly amazing that it nearly matched the joy and awe of the birth of her grandchildren. And, most importantly, would she have ever believed that she was more than enough? That she was worthy of so much love, joy, success, and happiness. She just had to first create a life that supported a healthy Cape before she would be ready to share that life with another—a partner for the rest of her life.

"Can I try to paddle now, Gramma?"

Her granddaughter's sweet voice pulls her out of her musing. She looks up to realize that the water is suddenly much calmer. The expression on her sweet Little Love's face is one of excitement, anticipation, and daring energy. Fearless—just like her gramma.

Now kneeling on the board, she pulls her standing Little Love back against her so they can balance together. Holding on to the oar horizontally in front of Little Love, she encourages her to grab hold of the oar where she had been taught. Dipping down into the water—first to the right, then down to the left—the four hands work together to move the oar back and forth, steering the board calmly through the water. Gramma Amy only wishes someone could capture a photo of this scene. She knows it will forever be imprinted in her memory—another experience patch on her Cape.

Little Love is so focused on moving the oar that she doesn't realize Gramma has taken her hands off. As they approach the island, Little Love giggles at how quickly the board has moved across the water. They are nearly to the island.

Suddenly, Gramma Amy gasps in surprise, making Little Love freeze and stop paddling. Trying not to lose her balance and fall in the lake, she carefully turns around to see her Gramma's face. "Gramma, what's wrong?"

With her right hand, Gramma grabs the weight of the oar out of Little Love's hands. But it is what Gramma's holding in her left hand that makes Little Love gasp. Her fingers are wrapped around the edges of a little blue Cape that is tied around the neck of Little Love.

"Well, honey, it seems you've found it."

Little Love stares in awe, grasping the edge of her very own little Cape of Courage. Gramma had always encouraged her to believe that she too could discover her own magical Cape—just as her mom had and her gramma before her.

As Little Love absorbs the reality of a Cape draped around her neck—her own unique superpowers ignited—Gramma witnesses Little Love change oh so subtly. Little Love suddenly looks not quite so little anymore. She stands more confidently—taller in both stature and presence. Her head tilts slightly up, exuding a quiet confidence. She seems to be relishing in the magic that she is.

As quickly as it arrives, the expression changes, and she is once again the excited little girl—huge smile and boisterous laugh—hugging her gramma. "Gramma, is my Cape waterproof?"

Gramma laughs. "It can be whatever you want it to be."

As Little Love screams with joy and prepares to jump into the water to celebrate, for just a moment, Gramma Amy sees it—the uncanny resemblance. She is reminded of another Little Love preparing to dive off a starter block so many years before. They have the same smile, Little Amy and Little Love. Gramma Amy recognizes and marvels at the genes…and the magic. That confident capability, the daring determination, the zest for life. The same desire to live like the hero of their own story. Each living fearlessly—with their Capes, of course.

Gramma Amy simply smiles. She is so grateful that her grand Little Love did not require a traumatic event to discover her Cape. She simply needed a Cape coach who could guide her journey to manifest a Cape of Capability, Courage, and Confidence.

With great pride and love, she watches Little Love swim around the paddleboard screaming, "I have a Cape! I have a Cape!"

For however longer she had left to live, Gramma Amy would continue to thank her younger selves for never giving up. The magic of this moment was worth every single low moment in her own life. Every single depressing rejection and redirection. Every time she doubted herself, her self-worth, and her capabilities. Thank God, she finally recognized that she had not made it to midlife only to give up her Cape for the second half of this life of hers.

And now, Gramma, Writer, Athlete, Mother, Auntie, Bestie, and Adventure Amy was busy living her most authentic life. On any given day, her uniquely Amy smile could magically be found playing a round of golf, taking her grandkids and dogs to the park, playing pickleball with friends, or teaching her grandkids how to grow a vegetable garden.

Nothing before had prepared Amy, or the Cape, for the joy of watching her granddaughter discover her own Cape. And she knew it was just the beginning of this particular kind of genetic magic. She couldn't wait to watch Little Love grow in her Cape. Become the hero of her own story...just like another Little Love so many years before.

Chapter 23

The Big, Audacious Dream

When everything felt out of her control during her reentry, Midlife Amy let her mind take her to a magical place in visualizing her future. She remembered that accessing her imagination was something she could control. Imagining her future chapters as Gramma Amy, she felt compelled to write. And it worked.

Reading her writing aloud, she sat back in her chair and smiled brightly—the sticky gray had fallen away from the Cape. Her own writing filled her with hope and helped her imagine her future self's options and potential. She felt inspired. And she wanted to keep writing.

She had loved to write, literally, for as long as she could remember. She had boxes of journals to prove it. Throughout the chapters of her life—highs or lows—she had written in her journals. In addition to a good sweaty run or a fun dance class, it was the activity that reliably ignited the authentic magic that lived inside of Amy's Cape.

From a young age, she found writing provided a safe place for her to process and organize her thoughts, express her feelings, and brainstorm ways to improve her situation. And to do all of that without having to please or impress someone else. Her own words had provided comfort, as they embodied a loyal friend in whom she could confide.

Her journey to find Little Amy healed her in ways she could never have imagined. Her writing was critical to the evolution of her Cape and the feelings of determination and hope for Future Amy. And as she read her writing, she wondered, *What if I could help other little selves who are feeling lost in their adult bodies? Perhaps other adults have also forgotten their childhood Capes? Did their little selves also dream of being the heroes of their stories? What if I could share my journey and inspire them to embark on their own?*

She tried to imagine the story of her journey having the power to encourage someone else to look closely in the mirror and recognize their own Cape. To help them take the steps needed to find their sweet little self. To understand what kept them from living their most authentic life. To uncover what made them feel truly happy, daring, and fearless.

Perhaps they would have the courage and determination to resolve the stickiness and heavy fabric of life that had taken over their Cape. To unravel the adult inner layers to uncover what made their Capes so heavy. To show love and compassion for their younger selves by removing the heaviness and refreshing their Cape. To do whatever it took to help them imagine their future selves filled with possibilities and dreams—just as their little selves had lived.

She would love to ask them:

> What were the dreams of your little self?
>
> What traumas and responsibilities of life covered your Cape and made you need to fly to survive what pain or fear?

What are you afraid of? And why?

What pain, buried deep in your gut, do you continue to ignore?

What is holding you back from revealing the part of your little self that was free to be happy and carefree?

What if you could learn to care for your Cape in ways you have tried to care for others? Consider what you can release from the Cape. What no longer serves you?

What would help you calm your belly and reset your mind? Mend your Cape from sadness, rejection, and doubt? Repel the heaviness of other people's expectations? Grow the Cape's fabric with life experiences your future selves will live?

She imagined others being able to wear their Capes with pride and owning their amazing uniqueness. Knowing they are worthy and enough just as they are. And remembering that their younger selves are the keepers of their true hopes and dreams. Why not find them and get reacquainted?

Feeling purposeful and inspired, she knew what she *could* do—what she very much wanted to do. She was determined to make an old, audaciously big, and scary dream come true. She resolved, *If not now, then when?*

She pulled her old dictionary off the shelf in her office, charged her laptop, and began to imagine. Began to write.

For as long as she could remember, her big, audacious dream looked a little something like this:

Walking the streets of a busy city, she sees the sign for a local bookstore. She hastens her stride, eagerly passing the window to open the front door to the store. Scanning the shelves with a twinkle of anticipation in her eye, she takes in the new-releases promotional signs and the books stacked at the front tables.

Slightly to the right, perhaps, she sees it. Her book. And not just one, but multiple copies of Future Amy's published book sit on display. She picks up the book, relishing the feel and weight of the hardcover copy. Then she opens to the front page and grabs a pen out of her purse. One by one, she signs her name inside the front cover of each copy on the shelf. When she is finished, she gently puts the books back on the shelf and places her pen in her purse, smiling beneath her sunglasses.

It was a dream that Little Amy had confidently assumed she would achieve—of course, she would. And this big dream had lived on through each of her younger selves. Every time she walked into a bookstore, no matter the stage of her life, she smiled at the vision of her secret dream. *Someday,* she would think.

Yet, the older she grew, the dreams of her children and those she had for them lived at the forefront of her mind. And it wasn't until she found herself in a bookstore, reading a book to her children, that the old dream returned. Yet, sadly, it was quickly covered with the doubts of a woman who believed there was no time for her own dreams.

As is often true about the dreams of adults, Amy couldn't imagine a time when she would have the energy and confidence to pursue her audaciously big old dream. Like many adults, she had lost confidence in her capabilities. Her Cape had been covered by imposter syndrome.

But Newly Awakened Midlife Amy uncovered the magic beneath the inner layers of her Cape. And her childhood dream that lived on with Little Amy. It persisted… just as Amy had. She just needed to activate the magic and believe in Future Amy to bring it to life.

And while that imposter syndrome—self-doubt and fear of rejection—relentlessly tried to entrench itself on her Cape, Amy wrote anyway. And she wrote fearlessly. She knew that if she didn't try, she would never know. And her future selves were counting on her to act…*now*. She didn't want to age with her what-ifs. She would rather know and fail than to always wonder. And she was a girl who tried. She had always been that girl. *So why wouldn't I try now?*

From the moment that she reframed her reentry, let go of the fear and doubt to focus on what she could control, her passion and purpose were activated. The magical thread on Little Amy's Cape ignited once more. She still didn't know what she would do for work in her next chapter, but she had lots of skills, lots of ways to earn money. She felt confident she would find a way.

In the meantime, Amy was healthy, alive, and thriving—living as if she were the hero of her own story. And a hero can do anything they believe is possible…with the magic of confidence, courage, and possibilities.

Wearing her refreshed Cape and practicing the daily care habits, she felt capable and determined. For the first time in a very long time, she was making time to focus on her dream. Writing for herself, first and foremost—but, hopefully, to also help others.

Amy Sue Irvine at the Fearless Girl Statue in New York City, New York, April 2018.

Eventually, and with great determination and magic, Writer Amy completed her book. Yet, it would take some of her greatest courage to share it with the world. And, she wore a Cape of Courage, after all. She finally set her story free and published it for the world to read.

In fact, you just finished reading it.

She hopes you feel inspired to find your own little self and activate his or her dreams. Learn to love yourself just as you are. Dare to live the rest of your life with a Cape of Courage to tackle the what-ifs and why-nots. Live like the hero of your own story.

The Epilogue

The journey to find Little Me began in 2019 after a total hysterectomy landed me in fight-or-flight survival mode. The surgery was the last step in my breast-cancer treatment. My cancer was hormone-receptor positive, so at forty-seven years old, I chose to shut down the hormone factory. Several organs were removed, and the physical recovery was intense. But the impact of the sheer-cliff drop in hormone levels was similar to no hell I could have ever imagined.

Following the surgery, the instant menopause sent my body and mind into a state of shock. My cortisol levels skyrocketed. There was no pill or therapy that could calm the intense changes in my body—I couldn't take hormone replacement therapy since it was the hormones that had caused my cancer.

No one seemed to have a clue how to help me. And a few months in, I was diagnosed with lymphocytic colitis, an acute condition caused by my body's fight-or-flight response. I was a total mess and beyond desperate for help. At my therapist's recommendation, I scheduled an appointment with an integrative holistic health doctor. It turned out to be the most amazing gift—and it absolutely led to you reading this book.

During my first appointment with this doctor, I received a prescription that would change my life forever. While on my way out of the room at the end of my appointment, the very kind doctor stopped to take my hand and calmly said, "Amy, when you go home today, all I want you to think about is what does Little Amy need?"

It took me several seconds to process what she said. Staring at the doctor, beginning to digest her words, I suddenly burst into tears. "What do you mean? Who is Little Amy? I have no idea who she is. So how could I possibly know what she needs?"

The doctor smiled, then reached out her hand to touch my arm, as one would comfort a child. She gave me a long hug, repeated her prescription, and sent me on my way home. I left her office dumbfounded and spent the next year contemplating how in the world I could find Little Amy.

Then the COVID-19 pandemic hit the world, and I found myself in an even deeper spiral of survival mode. How could my fragile lungs survive this horrible virus? And then the slow, quiet crash happened. Yet another situation I couldn't control. And my Cape felt unbearably heavy.

My depression was too tricky and at times very scary. I forgot who Amy was, let alone Little Amy. I knew clearly in my gut that my future self could not exist if I wasn't able to take the advice of that wise holistic doctor.

I imagine you have figured out by now that the Cape was actually just my imagination. It was all in my mind. It is, in fact, how I think of my mind...and my spirit, my soul. And as a result of this journey, my Cape feels incredibly healthy, balanced, and determined, once again. Not every day...but many days. Like my younger selves.

During my search to discover little me, I was able to clear my mind of the gray and heaviness to make way for the voices and emotions of my younger selves. This allowed me to recognize what really makes me tick at my core. What truly matters and brings me happiness and joy. What made my younger selves, and makes my current self, feel authentically me.

Reuniting with my younger selves, I remembered how much I loved to run, jump, dance, and play—yes, read and write, too. I recalled that I was daring and curious. And how easy it used to be for me to dream and *imagine*, and then concoct a daring plan to make that dream a reality.

I remembered that, as a young girl, I dared to think of myself as Wonder Woman—capable, fierce, and helpful.

(*Cue the original* Wonder Woman *theme song.*)

And even more importantly, I recognized the things that no longer, or never really did, bring me happiness, joy, or authenticity. Things that I tolerated and made the best of throughout my life. Things I simply just settled for or without. But they weren't really what I would've chosen for myself or my little selves.

But thanks to my group-therapy experience, this recovering people-pleaser finally learned the concept of boundaries. Better late than never! I finally adopted the practice of setting boundaries around the people, behaviors, and thinking that drains and no longer serves me. I chose to no longer give those things my energy or focus. Gave myself permission to say no.

As a result of my journey, I've reached the end of tolerating anything unhealthy for my Cape...my mind...and my body. I have little desire to prove anything to anyone, including myself. This new way of thinking, in itself, is likely the most incredible transformation and gift of my life. I breathe so much easier without having to constantly feel on.

Through the eyes of my younger selves, I found a magnified view of how very hard I had always been on myself. While I was being so generous, helpful, and forgiving of others, I was also acting as my own worst critic. I saw clearly the reasons why I had felt such doubt and unworthiness as I grew older. I recognized how life had impacted my confidence, had forced me to survive when I naturally just wanted to smile and imagine a better future.

And putting so much pressure on myself meant that I took myself way too seriously. The challenge in wearing a Cape is thinking that you have to take care of everything. No one ever told me I was wrong. That I get to decide how I want to use my Cape. And for a time, I did have agency over my choices. Those early adulting years when I used the Cape confidently, with daring and courage. But that agency turned to responsibility and obligation when I felt forced to use the Cape to take care of everyone else. When I used the Cape simply to survive my own superhero identity.

My driving goal in this journey was to understand how to spend the rest of my life thriving, instead of being caught in the spiral of a survival mindset. To achieve this meant coming to terms with my fears, the big pivotal moments and decisions I have faced, and the plot twists. Those unexpected twists in the ongoing plots of our lives. They force us to react and pivot, switch gears, even when we are happy with the current plot. They are often not fun at all, but they are typically the character-building events of our lives. They further the plot of our life story—and certainly keep it from being boring.

While living through my journey, I could never have imagined how this story would eventually come together. At first, I wanted to write about the Cape with a young-reader audience in mind. Teach about social and emotional learning through the story. However, as I began to find my little self—in the context of a mourning bird launcher—I knew I needed to understand my Cape first. To learn how to listen to my own needs and allow each version of myself the space to heal. Once I wrote for myself and my peers, perhaps then I could transfer the lessons to a younger audience.

While I attempted to weave together each unique chapter of plot twists and pivotal moments into a connected story, various themes emerged:

Healing from trauma and abandonment

Their impact on one's self-worth and self-love—never feeling enough. Once I began to heal from my traumas and abandonment, I found that feeling enough is pretty simple. It was really a matter of relearning how to talk to myself. When I catch my old critical inner self emerging, I shut her down. Of course, it happens still—I'm human, after all. I just practice my new favorite phrase: *Well, of course, you feel that way.* It allows me to validate and process emotions, then move forward. I use it with myself and others, and see their visible sighs of validation.

Decision-making with a "can" versus "should" question

I find this difference to be between capability and obligation. We all a choice in how we react to being asked for something. We do our best in every situation. In the future, we can ask ourselves, *Am I capable of doing this? Or is this something I feel obligated to do?* And then ask yourself, *What will best serve me authentically? What do I really want or desire to do?* The can-versus-should litmus remains a tool I use with myself during times of choice and indecision.

The proverbial empty nest versus reframing it as the bird launcher

I'm talking about the season after you've raised baby birds and set newly adult birds free into the world. If you've lived this or are in the throes of it, I'm sure you have asked yourself, *Now what?* The concept of an empty nest sounds pathetic. For those who have built their lives quite happily around their children, this loss can feel crushing. And even if we have done a good job of leading a balanced life while being an active parent, the change is still huge. It's a change in habits, social life, size of grocery orders, number of mouths to feed, and more. Weekends previously packed with kids' activities give way to Saturday mornings free for yoga classes and coffee with friends.

What do we do with the rest of our lives, when we were focused on the health and safety and job of raising the birds to adulthood? I, for one, hope you bird launchers feel inspired to find your little selves. Return your focus inward, finding inspiration from your own dreams.

Remember who you were and who you want to be when you grow up. You are worthy enough to launch yourself, too.

Parenting the Cape is no easy feat, but bird launchers are wise and skillful people. Why not turn that nurturing onto yourself? Parent your own Cape in the ways that you uniquely understand your personally needs.

Fear-versus-Growth Mindset

Allow yourself to unwind from obligations and responsibilities, and become fearless in taking calculated, daring risks for yourself. What do you dare to try? What's stopping you?

I began this journey by channeling the fearless girl who I imagined was Little Amy. I had to really understand why people, across the generations of Amy, had called me fearless. And what did that actually mean for me and my future? It's okay to feel afraid. The challenge, as we age, is in proceeding with our goals and dreams, despite the fearful feelings. I know for sure that feeling fearless means acknowledging the fear without allowing it to keep me from doing the what-if that I'm really curious about. For example, writing this book.

Change is hard

Living into my empty nest as a bird launcher remains one of my hardest changes yet—likely because I didn't expect to be single when it happened. For a hot minute after my son left for college, I had a partner, and we had a lot of fun.

But that unraveled after the slow, quiet crash, leaving me with me, myself, and I...and, well, the dog and cat, too!

The very, very quiet house left me with too much change all at once and way too many choices to make by myself. Changes that deserved attention in their own bird-launcher story. I had spent so many years taking care of others that I didn't know how to listen to my own needs. And I had forgotten how to imagine.

How did I manage the change? One day at a time. Sometimes five minutes at a time.

To change that state of my Cape, it took unraveling decades of a people-pleasing mindset and reacting to life in real time. To trust that I didn't have to always be ready for the worst to happen and show up prepared to be the hero. That I could accept the current state of my life in order to imagine the future that would bring me joy, happiness, and peace. That I could trust the process of digging in deep to reach the core of myself.

The refocusing on myself felt, at times, like my most treacherous change. But it was absolutely essential and worth it. Because I am worth it, and so are you. And whatever change you are going through now, before you know it, you'll be living into a new normal. Believe in yourself; live into the change process. Believe in the caterpillar's future.

Be kind to yourself—you've never done this before

The biggest surprise to me, in my journey to find Little Me, was how much compassion and love I would feel for her. For my younger self. When you, as an adult, get to know your younger self, you can't help but feel the need to be kinder to yourself. To treat yourself as you would other people you love. And when you love yourself, you realize that you're never really alone. Such a gift to finally see yourself as enough in your own eyes. To love yourself as you already are.

Uncovering your superhero's magic

Did the younger you ever imagine being a superhero? Why did that dream have to end with your childhood? Maybe you have lived some of your dreams, but why stop there? If you are a parent, perhaps you dreamed through the possibilities of your children? But why shouldn't your older selves get to keep dreaming, too?

Consider your own big, audacious dream... What is it? How can you ignite the magic on your Cape and give it a try? Why would you want to spend your life living with the what-ifs? Why sit out those pivotal moments? Make a choice. It's your choice, after all.

The journey to truly understand my Cape was far from easy. I fought countless bouts of doubt and too many episodes of major depression. For the last year alone, I was unemployed, drew upon my savings, and spent as little as possible. But I'd trained for the lifestyle when I was a starving college kid and a single mom on a limited income. I made choices.

And I certainly had many moments in which I almost gave up—both on my big, audacious dream and on my future. The critic absolutely took over the Cape. She spewed doubt, fear, and shame:

What was I going to do with the rest of my life?
Where was this writing going to take me?
Why would anyone even want to read it?
Would I end up feeling courageous enough to share it with anyone?

But without a plan B or even a Y, I had reached my plan Z. I had invested so much time and energy in my journey—too much to just leave it sitting on the shelf. I was determined to start living with the duality of the Cape. To find a balance between the overachiever and the loving, compassionate selves.

I had had enough of letting the critic's voice drive my fears, my doubts, my inactions. Sure, Aimee can also be a protective voice redirecting me based on gut feelings and past experiences. That contrary voice is important at times. But I tried to imagine what life would feel like if I abandoned my dream. What would Little Amy say? What did Little Amy need? By now, you know she needed me to make this dream come true. And I just couldn't disappoint her.

And after one corporate job rejection too many, I redirected my focus. I had had enough. For once in my life, I chose to bet on myself. I trusted my gut that said, *Amy, you have to try. You deserve to try. You have to know what you're made of.* I had always been a storyteller. Maybe, just maybe, I could help someone else. Isn't that what Little Amy always hoped to do?

And so I wrote. Along the way, I gave myself space to invite the heaviness of doubt into the forefront of my mind. I channeled enough courage to feel some very deep, painful emotions. I sat with shame, regret, sadness, and the hardships my younger selves faced. I gave them the compassion and love that I couldn't offer myself at the time. And contrary to what I had always feared, I didn't lose myself in the hard feelings. Instead, it was there that I found myself.

I have had too many dark nights in which depression came in with its sneaky voice, telling me that life was too hard. That it wasn't worth being in the pain that I felt. Sneaky depression…it really is a liar (thanks, Li). And yet it is a real state of mind and body for so many of us. For me, it was the gray cloud and sickness on my Cape.

I discovered that boundaries, exercise, sunlight, human connection, and the joy of a dance party are critical to blowing away the gray from my Cape. When I feel that I am enough as I am, I live in a place that recognizes the gray before it dares to carry me into the dark. I see it coming. I greet it and try to listen to why it has arrived. *What's going on with my Cape, my mind?*

I will likely always struggle with depression. I've accepted what I once thought of as my weakness—my kryptonite—as just a part of who I am. It clearly does have the potential to take me down. But when you accept something, it sure feels less likely to surprise you.

The gray has become just a part of me—something I expect to feel and recognize sometimes on my Cape. I no longer get furious with the gray, and I know what to do when it appears. I know to pull strategies from my mental health toolbox. If I start to feel gray, I force my Cape to carry me outside, move my body, grab a book, text a friend, or just go to bed. Do something, anything, that brings me joy. And the gray usually dissipates—the fog usually burns off, eventually. And the sunshine returns.

My newly refreshed Cape has been fortified by five decades of wisdom accumulated while living a full, complicated human life. I can approach life fearlessly, drawing upon the wisdom of my past doing and trying. When faced with a plot twist or challenge, I tell myself, *Remember, we've been here before. We've felt this and seen this. We survived before, and we will again.* Or even better, *We've been here before. Remember, we thrived! We can do it again.* It's the wisdom to know that whether my tries are for surviving or thriving, I will be okay. I can do both. It's only one chapter in the plot of my life.

We get to live this complicated journey that ultimately tells the story of a life well lived. We all have the capacity to be the hero of our own stories, regardless of how we are brought into the world. We all have the ability to dream, no matter the severity or ease of our life circumstances. Our influences, positive or negative, certainly impact the content of our dreams and the extent of our imaginations. But we are all born with unique gifts that make us authentically ourselves. And we get to choose how we will live into our characters, grow them, and fine-tune them as we discover who we are really capable of being.

I don't claim to have the recipe for a so-called perfect life. One that straddles the extremes of selfishness and altruism. We are all human, after all—no one is perfect. Finding a healthy sense of self-worth seems to be a nefarious undertaking. As I type this, I struggle to balance self-care with helping others—and likely will for the rest of my story.

But I have learned that just consciously striving for this balance ignites and sustains the magic in my Cape. Living true to my inner magic. Trusting my intuition, my inner self or gut. Those things seem to be the keys to living my most authentic life as the hero of my own story.

During my Midlife Awakening, I was able to heal the wounds that Little Amy never could. I accepted myself as *enough* just as I am—kryptonite and all. By embracing what I thought was my weakness, I found the magic that can come with engaging others for help. My strong, experienced, and resilient mind—my imaginary superhero Cape—activated the courage to live fearlessly into the new chapters of my life. Because I finally learned the most important magic of all—loving myself. And that means Little Amy, Little Adult, College Aim, Super Mommy, Single Mom, Writer Aim, and Grandma Amy.

It was worth it all. Because I'm worthy of healing, growing, and shifting into a healthier version of myself. And so are you.

I hope you enjoyed reading my story. May you feel inspired to dream and soar with courage and imagination, just as your little selves did before adulting brought responsibility, expectations, and obligations. May you find the magic of your little selves and fly with your own Cape of Wonder, Possibility, and Courage.

I hope you truly love your Cape and prioritize its care. Build habits to help it clear away any heaviness or stickiness that keeps you from living your best life. You are more than worthy of being the hero of your own story. Why not get started now?

Acknowledgments

I certainly would not be the person I am today without the incredible support of my family and friends. Acknowledging every single person who has contributed to the evolution of Little Amy would be impossible. I will, however, do my best to highlight the key players across the *Eras of Aim*. If I have forgotten your name, please forgive me.

First, my immense gratitude goes to these early readers for their thought partnership, collaboration, and encouragement: Susan Agnew, Randy Agnew, Margot Cook, Dawn Miller, Sarbjit Nahal, Niki Reina-Guerra, Zulima Davis, Lisa Carlock, Dan Brown, Amy Bradburn, Mariah Hay, and Sarah Doss. Thank you for believing in my writing and my journey, and for giving me the confidence to keep going, especially when my inner critic got in the way.

Very special thanks to Margot Cook, my career twin and dear friend. Your very early feedback on my manuscript and its potential impact on the lives of others made all the difference. You have virtually held my hand and cheered me on throughout the entire process. Thank you for your friendship, wisdom, and love.

This book and my journey to find Little Amy would not have been possible without my mom, Susan, and my brother, Randy. Thank you cannot begin to express my gratitude for your rock-solid presence in my life and for always having my back. This book is the culmination of a lifetime of being loved by you two. It's yours as much as it is mine.

Mom, thank you for being my Wonder Woman. You defied so many people's expectations and raised Randy and me on your own—quite remarkably, if I do say so myself. You taught us loyalty and the importance of traditions (Go Raiders and A's), the art of throwing a great party, and a love of artichokes and guacamole (not together!). And, most importantly, you showed us what it means to truly love your family. Thank you for your never-ending confidence in our capabilities and your expert sports cheerleading across multiple generations. I am grateful to be the daughter of such a remarkable woman, and grateful for everything you have done for me and the kids.

Randy, my lifelong best friend, is the bravest, kindest person I know. And I'm the lucky one who gets to call him my little brother. Thank you for always being my biggest fan—even when you had every right to be bugged by my overachieving. We may have missed out on a strong male role model, but you, my dear brother, absolutely exceeded even our greatest ideas of what a rock-star father could be. I am immensely proud of you. You are my personal hero, and I love you so much.

To my baby birds, Emily and Colby, thank you for bringing so much joy and happiness to my life. You are truly the best of me, and my pride in you has no end. Thank you for trusting in my decisions and for working so hard to make your own good choices. Your Capes are so very powerful, capable, and loved—it is my greatest joy to watch you fly.

To Drew and Adie, thank you for loving my kiddos. I am so grateful that they get to do life with you, and so happy that you are such a big part of our family and future.

To my gram, Phyllis Fisher—and GG to my kids, nephew, and nieces. A few years ago, when she was in hospice, I filled the silence one afternoon by reading her an early version of *The Cape*'s first chapters. After several minutes of narrating from my cell phone, I felt silly and stopped reading. I looked down to discover that Gram had opened her eyes. Staring at her in disbelief—*Can she really hear me?*—I held her hand and proceeded to read the story of Little Amy...*her* Little Amy. She closed her eyes peacefully. Thank you, Gram, for always listening to my stories and believing in my magic.

A huge thanks to the rest of my small but mighty family who helped raise Little Amy: Grandpa Ken and Great-Grandma Em; my aunt and uncle, Nancy and Grant Fisher, and my dear cousins, Melissa Davis and Michael Fisher. Thanks to my stepmom, Kaye Tigert, and my half-brother, Daniel Tigert. To Jim and Susie McKnight, who have always been like an aunt and uncle to me. And I couldn't forget all of the wonderful neighbors who watched Randy and me grow up on Whitney Court in Walnut Creek, California.

For my sister-in-law, Jenny, whom I've been lucky to know since she and Randy were eighteen years old and met in the dorms at Chico State. I am immensely proud of the life you two have built together. I feel so lucky to get to be Aunt Amy to Gannon, Alexa, Sabrina, and Brooke.

A girl doesn't get far in life without her girlfriends. To my tribe, my dearest besties, spanning my early adulting through my midlife awakening: Lisa Carlock, Kelly Moore Lawyer, Sarbjit Nahal, Niki Reina-Guerra, and Zulima Davis. This book wouldn't have happened without you and your presence in my life. Thank you for being, among countless different roles, my pledge sister, my historian, my teaching partner, my ride to radiation, my plus-one, my therapist, my comic relief, and my never-ending source of joy, laughter, and love.

Huge thanks to my dear friends and teammates throughout elementary and high school, especially Jennifer Tobey, Jeannine Long Barbato, Pam Colucci Larson, and their families. My high school besties, especially Trisha Pali, who always made me feel as if I really was Ms. Supersensational. And to Jim Holcomb, for teaching me that I really was lovable, after all.

Big thanks to my fourth-grade teacher, Kathleen Shea, who always believed that I could soar "To the Top!" Her husband, Pete Shea, the trailblazing basketball coach who had no problem drafting three girls to his team. My gratitude to the English teachers who nurtured my love of writing, especially Vicki Rodgers Hackett and Paul Dalmas. And the athletic coaches who encouraged this tomboy's tenacity and sportsmanship, especially Char Teutschel and Mrs. Inez Gussy.

My love and gratitude goes to all of my Alpha Phi sorority sisters from the Epsilon Rho chapter at the University of California, Davis, especially Jennifer Hilbert, Kelly Moore, Michelle Edmonds, and Lisa Taylor…all my love and AEO. To the Arkfelds: Dan, Cathy, Alison, Emily, and Matthew—thank you for being my college family. To my wonderful friends from my freshman-year dorm, Struve II, especially Trushita Patel, Jack Kleine, and Scott Gulstine. Also, many thanks to Dale Noleroth, Brad Cole, Brent Sasaki, and Tod Stolz for enjoying early adulthood with me.

I want to express my gratitude to those who lived my early-adulting years with me, especially Matthew Irvine. We were fortunate to learn how to parent and raise our "littles" with a huge, wonderful village in Davis, California. While there are countless wonderful parents and families from soccer teams (including the dozen I coached), baseball teams, and Applegate Dance Studio, special gratitude for their presence and support goes to: Lisa and Chad Carlock, Jennifer and Bob Hagedorn, Beverly and Bob Schacherbauer, Cherie and Patrick Archibeque, Kim and Kevin Bryan, Lola Cook, Grace and Chad DeMasi, Krista and Carson Wilcox, Betsy Levine, Kerry and Jim Hickerson, Samantha Fusselman Villarreal, and Alison and Stan Kennedy. And special thanks to Mike Bryner and the crew at Lamppost Pizza in Davis, for countless Friday nights spent with four generations of family, pizza, beer, and great friends.

Our life in Davis wouldn't have been the same without the tremendous support and love of the staff, families, and students at Patwin Elementary School. Thank you to every single teacher and staff for influencing my children—you know who you are, and we love you. You created such a truly magical place for me and my kids to grow. I'm especially appreciative to those who helped me bring Teacher Amy to life: Sarbjit Nahal, Kate Bowen, Michelle Flowers, Linda Biewer-Elstob, Mary Talyn, Marcia Houston, Leslie Zais. I will always remember Patwin as the place where I did my very best work. Go Hawks!

And for my beloved fifth-grade students in Room 21 at Patwin Elementary School in Davis, California, who knew a lot about my big, audacious dream. Mrs. Irvine did it! Now, go make your dreams come true!

I will always be grateful to the dear people who helped Single Mom survive and Midlife Amy awaken, especially the wonderful families of Elk Grove, California, who warmly welcomed my littles and me during our big, scary move. My sincerest gratitude and love goes to Greg Staby, Joe Nefsky, Susan Hopkins, Kendra Blanchette, Jennifer Hart, Bill Briggs, Tara and Trevor Ferruggia, Michele and Derrick Rebensdorf, Dan Ammann, Niki and Kevin Dimond, and Stacy and Tom Rehman. Special thanks also to the women and coaches of Kaia Fit Laguna-Elk Grove. And to all of the many families and coaches whom we spent countless weekends and evenings with, especially Colby's youth baseball and all-star teams, and his FC Elk Grove Heat soccer team.

And I couldn't forget my coaches and gym besties at Laguna Creek Sports Club. Thank you for helping Midlife Amy get her fitness and game back…and especially for reminding me how much I love to dance.

I also want to acknowledge all of my work family and professional colleagues who experienced life with me while we grew, raised our families, and contributed to our company's success. Special thanks and appreciation go to: Dawn Miller, John McGehee, Ivonne Smith, Molly Scholes, Margot Cook, Calvin McKnight, Suzanne Vlahos, Holly Bowden, Samantha Olsen, Jill Bailey, Dale Fitzgerald, Mike Knudtsen, and my entire Amy Strong family at Pluralsight. And to my wonderful global teammates at Salesforce. We lived through a pandemic together, yet found ways to achieve so much and have a ton of fun. Can you believe I turned my pivotal moments into a book?

For Doug Nowak, who brought joy, laughter, and love into my life in the time of COVID-19. And to my therapists and peers for supporting my journey to the other side of my slow, quiet crash—especially Brandon Baker.

Huge thanks to Katherine (Kate) Haff for illustrating the five lovely sketches at the beginning of each "Part" of the story. Thank you for sharing your talents with me and my readers.

And, finally, to Phil Sakoi, Ryan Wells, and the incredible team at Dos Coyotes Border Café in Elk Grove, California. Thank you for feeding me, cheering me on, and giving me a place to activate my creative magic. Your delicious food, smiles, and encouragement for Writer Aim meant the world.

Let's Connect

If you want to learn more about Amy, visit her website at www.amysueirvine.com, sign up for her blog, and learn what's new from The Cape Consulting.

Email Amy at:
AuthorAmyIrvine@gmail.com

Instagram:
amyirvineauthor

Facebook:
Amy Irvine Author

www.ingramcontent.com/pod-product-compliance
Lightning Source LLC
Chambersburg PA
CBHW060124170426
43198CB00010B/1018